Jimi Clay
1980
Gold

Praise for *Gold Medal Strategies*

"*Gold Medal Strategies, like* Jim Craig, is a true winner! Jim's successful Olympic and professional hockey career has put him in position to help companies produce gold medal teams. The book is perfect for our organization—a must read."
> —DAVID MASON, CEO, HEALTH CONNECT PARTNERS, INC.

"*Gold Medal Strategies* is a must read for any manager looking to build, develop, and energize a high-performance team for execution. Jim's pragmatic, straightforward approach has application for even the most seasoned executive!"
> —DON COLLERAN, EXECUTIVE VICE PRESIDENT, GLOBAL SALES, FEDEX

"*Gold Medal Strategies* is just what your sales team needs: firsthand insights on how teamwork, the value of preparation, goal setting, and developing a 'winning underdog' attitude can positively impact the success of your company."
> —JACK LAURENDEAU, VICE CHAIRMAN, ACOSTA SALES & MARKETING

"No one assimilates winning in business and sports quite like Jim Craig; his focus on goal achievement is easily related to and implemented, whether you are going for a gold medal or a victory in today's market. *Gold Medal Strategies* does it all."
> —TONY MEOLA, CEO, SAXON

"Jim Craig's critical role in the 'Miracle on Ice' in 1980 was the epitome of peak performance. Now he combines that experience with everything he has learned in business and in life over the past 30 years into another winning achievement. *Gold Medal Strategies* should be read by anyone who has a team."
> —DAVE OGREAN, EXECUTIVE DIRECTOR, USA HOCKEY

"There are no better lessons than those we learn from life, and no better example of that than Jim Craig and the 'Miracle on Ice.' *Gold Medal Strategies* fits all ages, and everyone learns from it."
> —BERNIE SWAIN, FOUNDER, WASHINGTON SPEAKERS BUREAU

"For years, Jim has seamlessly tied USA's 1980 'Miracle on Ice' success into smart business lessons in all of his corporate speeches. *Gold Medal Strategies* is no different. It is a business strategy must-read book."
> —DAVID SCHWAB, VICE PRESIDENT, MANAGING DIRECTOR, OCTAGON

"I have had the good fortune of watching Jim Craig reshape the attitude of a national sales force in just over an hour by weaving the parallel threads of business performance and hockey performance. Now his book *Gold Medal Strategies: Business Lessons from America's Miracle Team* gives anyone interested in lighting a fire under the organization a chance to see how it's done. Jim transfers the energy and entertainment of his personal appearances into the written word. I have seen the energizing effect he can have on a crowd, and those feelings of positive intent came back as I read through the book."

—STEVEN ROBINS, PRESIDENT, BAUSCH & LOMB VISION CARE
NORTH AMERICA

"On a long-ago Friday night, Jim Craig stood between the pipes of a little hockey rink in Lake Placid, New York, and delivered arguably the greatest performance under pressure in the annals of the Olympic Games, turning away 39 Soviet shots and forever redefining the parameters of athletic possibility. In these pages, Craig is no less on top of his game, offering page after page of profound insights and innovative strategies, showing us that winning in business and in life has a whole lot in common with achieving an Olympic miracle. It is a splendid piece of work."

—WAYNE COFFEY, AUTHOR

"Jim Craig provides inspiration and a playbook to create winning teams, from sports to business to elite military units. What makes his message unique is that it optimizes the talent and motivates the people to overcome any situation."

—MICHAEL MINOGUE, UNITED STATES MILITARY ACADEMY AT WEST POINT
GRADUATE; U.S. ARMY PLATOON LEADER, DESERT STORM

"Jim Craig's story and his message are both inspiring and educational. Jim addresses what is really important to achieve success. Creating a bold vision, holding fast to your convictions, moving forward with courage, having a passion and drive to succeed, silencing the naysayers, and achieving the mission—whatever it takes is what Jim teaches us in *Gold Medal Strategies*. It is a must read for all who want to achieve a gold medal in life."

—GARY CHARTRAND, EXECUTIVE CHAIRMAN, ACOSTA SALES AND
MARKETING COMPANY

"The winning underdog attitude is engaging and provides a strategic advantage: never underestimate the competition. In *Gold Medal Strategies*, Jim Craig incorporates strategies into a motivating presentation that encompasses winning—a subject he is very familiar with!"

—ROBERT DELUCA, SANOFI-AVENTIS

"Winning an Olympic gold medal was only the beginning of Jim Craig's journey to create a legacy and achieve victory in whatever he set out to accomplish. In his book, Jim shares with the reader his lifetime experiences and inspires others to look introspectively and 'pay it forward' for the benefit of future generations."

—TONY PINSONAULT, MANAGING PARTNER, PINSONAULT ASSOCIATES, LLC

"Jim Craig not only provides extraordinary insights (gleaned from his extraordinary life), but he has served as an inspiration to me and all my executives to 'go for the gold.' Jim has contributed significantly to the success of my business. With this book he can spread his valuable advice to a larger audience."

—IRA D. RIKLIS, PRESIDENT, SUTHERLAND CAPITAL MANAGEMENT, INC.

"Jim Craig is an amazing American sports icon who will forever be remembered for his role as a member of the 1980 U.S. men's Olympic gold medal hockey team. In his book *Gold Medal Strategies: Business Lessons from America's Miracle Team*, Craig manages to capture the spirit of his sports experiences and to represent them in a context that is entertaining, riveting, and beneficial for all who are tasked with leading and inspiring teams. It is a quick read, well worth the time."

—DENNIS R. MAPLE, PRESIDENT, ARAMARK EDUCATION,
ARAMARK CORPORATION

"Honeywell has brought Jim Craig in to speak at two of its corporate meetings. He did a standout job each time, not only inspiring and entertaining, but also teaching how the elements of teamwork that enabled the 1980 U.S. Olympic hockey team to be a world-beater and perform optimally can be practiced by Honeywell to continually improve and outperform the competition. In *Gold Medal Strategies: Business Lessons from America's Miracle Team*, you will find the lessons that Jim spoke about and taught when he addressed Honeywell, and more. The book is an immensely educational, motivating, fun, and valuable read."

—JOE PUISHYS, PRESIDENT, HONEYWELL INTERNATIONAL, ENVIRONMENTAL
& COMBUSTION CONTROLS

Gold
Medal
STRATEGIES

Gold
Medal
STRATEGIES
BUSINESS LESSONS FROM AMERICA'S MIRACLE TEAM

JIM CRAIG
AND DON YAEGER

WILEY

John Wiley & Sons, Inc.

Published by John Wiley & Sons, Inc., Hoboken, New Jersey.
Published simultaneously in Canada.

For general information on our other products and services or for technical support, please contact our Customer Care Department within the United States at (800) 762-2974, outside the United States at (317) 572-3993 or fax (317) 572-4002.

Wiley also publishes its books in a variety of electronic formats. Some content that appears in print may not be available in electronic books. For more information about Wiley products, visit our web site at www.wiley.com.

Library of Congress Cataloging-in-Publication Data:

Craig, Jim.
  Gold medal strategies : business lessons from America's miracle team / Jim Craig, Don Yaeger.
      p. cm.
  Includes index.
  ISBN 978-0-470-92806-6 (hardback); ISBN 978-1-118-02344-0 (ebk);
ISBN 978-1-118-02372-3 (ebk); ISBN 978-1-118-02373-0 (ebk)
  1. Management.   2. Leadership.   3. Organizational behavior.
4. Organizational effectiveness.   I. Yaeger, Don.   II. Title.
  HD31.C683 2011
  658.4'022–dc22

                                                          2010045657

Printed in the United States of America.

SKY10034455_051322

This book is dedicated to my wife, Sharlene, and our children, JD and Taylor; to my 1980 U.S. Olympic teammates; to all my hockey coaches, especially Herb Brooks, Jack Parker, and Craig Patrick; to my business and life mentors, Dan Pratt, Paul Haley, Dave Brandon, and Jon Luther; and to the Gold Medal Strategies team.

Thank you, all of you, for your love and friendship and support – and for pulling greatness out of me.

Jimmy

To Jeanette: Thanks for bringing a championship mindset to our family. You are my Gold Medal.   *DY*

CONTENTS

CONTENTS

I believe that everyone alive in America that February night in 1980 knows where they were. To me, and many others, it was the most memorable sporting moment in history. The images from the Lake Placid arena are burned into our brains. The fact that this group of young U.S. Olympians beat the unbeatable Russians was world-changing. Add to that the fact that these American heroes had to face and beat Finland two days later for the gold medal, and the whole thing was astonishing.

The image that had the most impact on me was watching Jim Craig seek out his father in the stands with the American flag draped over him. It brought chills and tears—chills because in that moment my confidence in the future of the United States was restored, and tears because I felt for the Craig family, who had just lost a wife and mother. My faith in family and values was solidified as well. Because of that, I always had a great deal of respect for Jim Craig, never believing I would ever meet him to share my thoughts with him on a personal basis.

But a miracle happened, and I met Jim Craig in 2003 when he did an appearance for Dunkin' Donuts where I was the CEO. I had heard he had grown into an inspiring and engaging speaker, and on that day he met expectations—and more.

What impressed me as well was that beyond fulfilling what was required of him, he was personable and provided a high level of individual attention to people at the event. As I got to know Jim better, I discovered that this warmth and caring quality was grounded and nurtured from growing up in a big, loving family. It confirmed what I had thought would be the character of the man. We became friends.

These character traits had been evident and strengthened the role he had performed as the goalie for the 1980 U.S. "Miracle on Ice" Olympic hockey team. Now I saw these traits demonstrated live. It was the close-knit and caring family paradigm that enabled the 1980 team—all the players and coaches recognizing that they were one family—to win gold at Lake Placid. You can't be a world-beater without compassion and concern for the people around you. You have to care deeply, and deeply believe in what you are doing.

This notion motivated and guided Jim in hockey—and it is carried through in his business pursuits and in life today.

Jim not only did appearances for Dunkin' Brands, but he also worked with us to develop profitable incentive and consumer promotions programs. As he does today in his keynote speaking and teamwork coaching, Jim approached each sales and marketing assignment as a separate challenge. He utilized precise elements of tactics and strategies, while staying true to the primary messages and values that are essential to a powerful and enduring brand. Jim is among the most talented and dedicated sales and marketing professionals with whom I have worked—and I have worked with many.

One of Jim's strongest suits is that he pays attention to the details that are important to success. He doesn't neglect the small stuff—and he sees the bigger picture as well. I suspect that may link back to his career in the net when he would have all the action on the ice in front of him—and he had to think many plays ahead to anticipate what could be coming his way.

I always relate to his strength of character, for that is what enables him to win in all arenas. Throughout my own career as a business leader, I have sought not only to build teams skilled in the Xs and Os of management, but also to select people with strong values who can role model these values to inspire others to succeed. Talent and intellectual horsepower get you in the game. When they are paired with honesty, humility, compassion, and passion, among other virtues, you win the game!

All of these qualities and virtues were necessary for Jim to play the role of the backbone, the final line of defense, for the 1980 U.S. Olympic hockey team—a group that demonstrated optimum teamwork and efficiency.

It is because Jim is made of such stalwart character that we became close friends. He is a devoted husband and father, and he has said many times, publicly and in writing, that in the final appraisal that is how he wants to be judged in terms of whether he was a winner.

Without question, his qualities as a person are pivotal to his success in motivating, teaching, and pulling greatness out of people and organizations, and to his overall success as an athlete and a businessman.

Typical of Jim, he is eager to give credit and thanks to all those who have helped him succeed. And I know he receives special gratification when he talks about his 1980 teammates and how they all worked together to, as Jim is fond of saying, "win the unwinnable and beat the unbeatable."

I have learned a tremendous amount from my friend Jimmy—and I am a better person for knowing him.

Enjoy this book and take counsel of its lessons. It is a trove of smart advice and wisdom; all delivered by a great athlete, a great person, a great American—and a consummate winner.

—Jon "Jack" Luther
Chairman of the Board, Dunkin' Brands

ACKNOWLEDGMENTS

There are so many people to whom I owe a huge debt of gratitude not only for this book, but for all the opportunities I've been given in life.

I'd like to start by thanking my wonderful parents: my mother, who toted me all over the greater Boston area for hockey practice and games while I was growing up, and my father, who was the backbone of our family after Mom died and my biggest fan. They have been the two greatest parents anyone could have, and my siblings and I are the luckiest kids on earth to have been born to into the crazy Craig clan.

My wife Sharlene ("Charlie") and our two amazing children are the proudest part of my life. The love and laughter that they give me every day overwhelm me when I think about what an incredible family I've been given.

Of course, I have to offer a huge thank-you to Ross Muscato, my longtime friend, business partner, and all-around great guy. Ross is truly someone without whom this book could not have happened. He is an incredible writer and his efforts to help me craft and refine my speeches over the years are really what laid the groundwork for this project. I am truly humbled that such a talented man would be willing to work alongside me, and I am grateful beyond words for his invaluable insight, ability, and friendship.

To Don Yaeger, whose knowledge of the book business and unending energy helped pull it all together, thank you.

Thank you, too, to the people at John Wiley & Sons for their belief in this book and the potential it has to inspire and excite all kinds of teams.

And, finally, I want to thank all of my teammates and coaches from the 1980 USA Olympic Hockey Team. You are the most amazing group of men I have ever had the privilege of knowing. Each of you has left an indelible mark on my life, and I am better for it. And to our head coach, Herb Brooks: You are sincerely missed every day. I hope this book makes you proud; you're the reason I was able to write it. From the bottom of my heart, thank you.

When ABC sportscaster Al Michaels bellowed those words—
"Do you believe in miracles?"—with about four seconds re-
maining in our game against the Soviet Union on Friday evening,
February 22, 1980, he gave to the sports world a phrase for the ages.
He also inspired the term "Miracle on Ice," which in turn inspired
the title of an HBO documentary, *Do You Believe in Miracles? The
Story of the 1980 U.S. Olympic Hockey Team*, and a Disney major
motion picture, *Miracle*. The word "miracle" is attached to what the
1980 U.S. Olympic team did in February 1980 in Lake Placid, New
York.

Miracles are inspiring; they give us hope, support the notion
that all is possible, and are the stuff of high-level drama. What we
accomplished on that sheet of ice in that village in the Adirondacks
in upstate New York was all of that. But it was not a miracle—even
if I believe in them. Highly improbable? Yep. Astounding? Maybe.
Shocking? You could say that.

But not a miracle.

What we accomplished at Lake Placid was the result of a lot of
hard work—and a lot of smart work. It was the result of exceptional
and brilliant mentorship. It was the result of sublime execution and
poise in competition. It was a result of one of the best demonstrations
of team chemistry in sports history.

Of course, what had, and what was going on in the world at the
time of our victory, greatly enhanced the chest-swell and feel-good
quotient of beating the Soviets and then, two days later, clinching
the gold medal with a win over Finland.

America was in a big funk—and had been for a while. Vietnam and Watergate were still very much open and sore wounds. Our economy was in a bad way; we were in a deep recession with high inflation and high unemployment. We had to deal with an energy shortage. So pervasive and gloomy was the mood in the land that on the evening of July 15, 1979, President Jimmy Carter delivered a primetime television address to the nation—which would later be popularly known as the "Crisis in Confidence Speech"—in which he spoke about what he called a "fundamental threat to American democracy," a threat, the president said, that "is nearly invisible in ordinary ways. It is a crisis in confidence. It is a crisis that strikes at the very heart and soul and spirit of our national will. We can see this crisis in the growing doubt about the meaning of our own lives and in the loss of a unity of purpose for our nation."

Things would get worse for our country.

On November 4, 1979, 66 U.S. citizens—63 working at the U.S. Embassy and three working at the Iranian Foreign Embassy in Tehran—were taken hostage by Iranian students and militants. Thirteen of the hostages were released by the end of the month, and another was released the following January. But 52 Americans would be held hostage for 444 days.

On December 27—with the Cold War already at Arctic temperature—Soviet troops invaded Afghanistan.

Uncle Sam was hurting at home. It couldn't rescue its hostages. It couldn't boot the Soviets out of Afghanistan.

The 1980 Winter Olympics in Lake Placid—which would open on February 13 and close on February 24—was set against this national and international angst, uncertainty, and fear. We were hosting an international festival, but there seemed to be little reason to smile and celebrate, even if big things were expected from American athletes like speed skater Eric Heiden, figure skater Linda Fratianne, and alpine skier Phil Mahre.

For sure, there were some smart hockey people who looked at the U.S. hockey team and recognized it was very good and could surprise people and maybe win a bronze medal. In those years, U.S. amateur hockey did not have a track record of success, and a third place in the Olympics would be a major accomplishment.

But as for the gold medal, it was certain that the Soviet hockey squad, a longtime powerhouse, would win it for the fifth consecutive Olympics.

The Red Army Team was a collection of some of the best hockey players on earth—amateurs in name only—who were also employees of the Soviet state and military. They trained hard, intelligently, and innovatively. The players worked together seamlessly and cooperatively, and together they played a game that was precise, elegant, fast, and highly effective. National Hockey League teams and NHL all-star teams faced the Soviets and got trounced.

An exemplar of the country and the military complex that sponsored it, the Soviet national team was mysterious and powerful. Its players wore plain red uniforms with CCCP (Russian for USSR) stitched on the front. Their faces showed little emotion—hardly ever a smile—as they dismantled opponents.

At Lake Placid—and on American ice—the Soviet hockey team would win a gold medal, and a battle in the Cold War, and the entire episode would make us feel even worse. To certify what the United States—and everyone else—was in for: Four days prior to the Opening Ceremonies of the games, we played the Soviets in an exhibition game at Madison Square Garden and lost 10-3. It wasn't good.

The next day in my hometown newspaper, *The Boston Globe*, sportswriter Peter Gammons commented on anti-Soviet political protests outside of Madison Square Garden the night of the game, and on the game itself: "Hockey is simply not the place for the evocation of political passion, not when it involves the Soviets. That was yesterday's first lesson. The second is that no one in the Olympics is going to challenge them.... As long as it's hockey, the Soviets will always have the last laugh in the Olympics. That they reminded us of yesterday."

Considering international hockey history and that a Soviet victory at Lake Placid was all but unanimously conceded and accepted, it is understandable what word came to the mind of Al Michaels and what he blurted through that headset. It was appropriate. It was also appropriate to exult in a group of American college kids that beat the big and bad Soviet Bear at a time when America desperately needed a victory.

Yet it didn't take a miracle to win the unwinnable and beat the unbeatable and to lift the spirits of a nation. The fact was we were a great hockey team, a collection of very good and great players, who operated under the mentorship of a great coach and his staff—and who together demonstrated teamwork for the ages. That we beat the Soviets and won Olympic gold was not a supernatural event—even if sometimes it seems that way.

I also remind people that our gold medal effort at the XIII Winter Olympic Games was not just about one game—but seven games. We won because of the teamwork we exercised and put forth in a thrilling last minute come-from-behind tie against Sweden, and in wins over Czechoslovakia, Norway, Romania, West Germany, the Soviet Union, and Finland.

We won because of proper preparation—and then focusing and playing our best hockey at the most important time. I am forever fortunate and blessed to be a member of that team.

Today my vocation—and avocation—is traveling the country, inspiring people and organizations, and teaching and coaching winning teamwork. The experience and examples of the 1980 U.S. Olympic hockey team are fundamental to the way I make a living—and they also play an integral role in the way I make my life.

It is immensely rewarding to help people and groups perform optimally and achieve their full potential. Through this book, I continue those efforts—and in it I hope you find motivation and guidance that will help you win your own gold medal and get to the top of your own victory podium . . . and, okay, even maybe create your own miracle.

1

Great Teams Think of Themselves as Winning Underdogs

> *It's David versus Goliath, and I hope we remember to bring our slingshots.*
>
> —**HERB BROOKS**, prior to the U.S.—Soviet game
> at the 1980 Winter Olympics

People remember that during the Olympics, the mask I wore had shamrocks on it—one on the right and one on the left, to the outside of the eye openings. The shamrocks were for luck, and also a nod of pride to my Irish heritage. During the 2010 Vancouver Winter Olympics, the U.S.A. starting goalie, Ryan Miller, played with a mask on which were painted Olympic and patriotic images—and also a shamrock, which I was honored to learn he had placed there as a tribute to me.

I am a mix of Irish and Scottish ancestry, with a bit more of my lineage weighted to the Irish side. My people came from the British Isles. Fundamental to my family history is something that is fundamental to the history of tens of millions in America: Leaving a place—a familiar place, even if at the time it was a place short on opportunity—and traveling to a place about which a lot had been read and talked about, a place that held great promise, yet no guarantees, and about which there was still a lot that was unknown.

You came to the United States because you were persecuted, hungry, and hoping for something better. Many came here because they had to escape something, or get away from someone or something, even the law.

You came with dreams—big dreams. You had big hopes. You believed you could defy the odds, do the seemingly impossible, even the miraculous.

And if you were one of those who got off the boat and were on your way to making a name for yourself, you stepped onto American soil with something to prove; you had a chip on your shoulder. You were a "winning underdog."

Peggy Noonan, author and newspaper columnist, former speech-writer for President Ronald Reagan, and a chronicler of the American experience, recognizes that people infused with the spirit and identifying themselves as a winning underdog made America great. In one of her *Wall Street Journal* columns she wrote, "Our people came here not only for a new chance, but to disappear, hide out, tend their wounds, and summon the energy, in time, to impress the dopes back home. America has many anthems, but one of them is 'I'll show "em!"'"

"I'll show "em!" is about being a winning underdog.

Great teams think of themselves as winning underdogs.

Kindle Your Competitive Fire

I am one of eight kids who grew up in a lower-middle-class family in North Easton, which is actually a village within the incorporated town of Easton. North Easton is located about 30 miles south of Boston. I had four older sisters; I was the third oldest of the brothers. My mom, Peg, and my father, Don—the man for whom I famously searched the stands at Lake Placid—were devoted, loving, and very warm people.

My father was a talented athlete (he is a member of the Oliver Ames High School Athletic Hall of Fame, the high school from which he graduated in 1936, and from which I graduated in 1975). He was a Big League prospect in baseball, and had a full athletic scholarship to attend Assumption College, but the very summer he was to head off to college, he seriously injured his hand while working in a factory. He did not go to college.

My father made most of the money coming into our household as the food service director at a local community college; he also worked part-time jobs, and volunteered on the town board of health for close to 30 years, as well as being a youth sports coach. He was busy. Yet not as busy as my mother who, as a homemaker with eight kids and our family's chief operations officer, worked around the clock.

Our home was small; it had one bathroom. When I speak to groups, a story that always gets a loud laugh—and if you are part of a big family, you laugh with understanding—is when I tell of how growing up in the Craig family, on those rare occasions when we had a steak dinner, if you had to get up from the table for anything—to answer the phone or go to the bathroom, whatever—then you took that steak dinner with you; because if you didn't take it with you, you could be certain that when you returned to the table, the steak would be gone, if not everything else on your plate as well.

We didn't have a lot, but we had enough. We were also a team. It was understood by us, and in town, that if you touched one Craig then you touched them all.

I was a kid and I was already indoctrinated in the "all for one" and "one for all" quality that enabled a group of guys, unheralded and underestimated, to one day make history in the Adirondacks. And soon I would have something to prove. I had attitude that kindled the fire—and I would become a winning underdog.

■ ■ ■

I was in fifth grade. It was 1968. Back then, Easton had three youth sports leagues: Little League, a church basketball league, and an ice hockey league. That was it, which in many ways I think is a good thing. (I am concerned that today we start kids in sports too early, and that they are overscheduled, but I won't go on about that here.)

I was already playing baseball; I was a catcher. I didn't play hoops, but our postman, Phil Thompson, told my parents that he thought hockey would be good for me. Smart guy, that Mr. Thompson.

I started out with borrowed skates; they were a little big so I put cardboard in the toes. I played goalie, because I liked the equipment; it looked similar to a baseball catcher's equipment. Plus, it seemed that the goalie didn't need to know the rules. No rules for the goalie—just stop the puck.

The young goalie – the dream begins. (Notice the baseball catcher's chest protector that Jim is wearing. Not long after this photo was taken, Jim's parents bought Jim a hockey goalie chest protector. "Money was tight," recalls Jim, "but my mom and dad said that I shouldn't be out there without the right equipment. So they bought me that goalie chest protector.")
Credit: Jim Craig

I was good—I could skate and had solid reflexes. I was also small—smaller than almost all the other kids in the league. Being small, though, didn't prevent me from dreaming big. I wanted to play in the Olympic Games. One time, in seventh grade, the teacher saw me not paying attention to her lecture; instead I was busy writing on paper. I was near the back of the class, and the teacher walked toward me and called out, "Jimmy, what are you doing?" I looked up and said, "I am practicing my autograph. I am going to be in the Olympics some day and people are going to want my autograph."

I was all of 12 years old, and already I had attitude and was kindling my competitive fire.

When I was still in junior high, almost every Sunday morning throughout the year, I used to travel into Boston with the older guys who were already playing hockey for Oliver Ames High School, the school I would soon attend. We traveled the 25 miles to Boston Arena (now Matthews Arena) so that we could play against the best high school and amateur talent around.

A car would pull into my family's driveway at about five A.M. Among the players I drove in to the city with were Ricky Bodio, Ray Daly, Peter Deibel, and Billy Condon. They were juniors and seniors at Oliver Ames, and since they were talented and tough athletes, I looked up to them figuratively; and, since at the time I was 5'1" and 120 lbs., I also looked up to them literally.

I would lug out my equipment, join the guys, and, all packed together, we were on our way. We got on the ice around 6 A.M. and put in a good five hours; sometimes we would play until noon. It was a sacrifice and tiring—but I also loved it. I would stay in net sometimes for four hours straight and take the best that the older players could dish out. I knew they were determined to break this little squirt in net, but I was just as determined not to fold. I wanted to prove to the older guys that I could hack the pressure and, if I was already in high school, that I could back them up. Just as importantly, I wanted to prove to myself that I could take it.

The practice paid off. I started for the varsity when I was a freshman. Yet I remained small. As a sophomore, come hockey time, I was all of 5'5" and 120 lbs. Yet even a few years prior to becoming a Boston University Terrier, I was already a terrier in practice in games; that is, I played with emotion, confidence, and attitude that were outsized for my frame. After practice ended, I stayed on the ice and had our assistant coach, Gerry Linehan, fire shot after shot at me.

I grew. My senior year, when I stood in net for the Oliver Ames Tigers, I was 5'10", 170 lbs. We lost only one game during the regular season, and we made it a couple games into the state tournament before losing to the eventual state champion. I made a couple of local newspaper all-scholastic teams, but I didn't make the big city newspaper teams at the *Boston Globe* and *Boston Herald*. Not one Division I college was interested in offering me a scholarship. I knew I could play at that level, but it seemed, with the exception of my mom and dad, no one else did.

As well, I had next to no concept of what was involved in applying for college. I had worked hard in the classroom in high school and done all right but not great in the grades department. I didn't do well on my SATs. I am not even sure if I took any Achievement Tests.

I wanted to go to college, but it seemed I wasn't prepared.

I mean, the application essays were daunting. And there were application fees. Just swinging the money to apply to college was going to be difficult.

But I got the break in the person of Mike Addesa, the hockey coach at the College of the Holy Cross, an independent NCAA Division I program. Mike had been a high school hockey referee who worked many games in which I played. He was impressed by what he saw, and he told me he thought I could play major college hockey. He helped with the process of applying to Holy Cross, and he told me that, provided I was accepted—which he said was just about guaranteed—I would receive a full athletic scholarship.

Things looked good. That was until I didn't get accepted at Holy Cross.

What now? I consulted and talked with my family and friends, and we felt that an excellent option would be to attend Norwich Academy, a military college in Vermont that had a Division III hockey program.

I applied and was accepted to Norwich. I arrived for the fall semester. I stayed at Norwich Academy for about two weeks. This wasn't a good fit. What confirmed that this wasn't the place for me was when an upperclassman came into my room, and in the mode of indoctrinating me took a framed photo of my mother, who was battling cancer, and threw it on the ground. I went at him—and I guess I wasn't supposed to. I said enough of this and headed back to Easton.

What now?

I needed to stay in school—and to continue studying and to continue playing hockey.

I enrolled at Massasoit Community College, in Brockton, the gritty city that borders Easton and is better known as being at one time the world's biggest manufacturer of shoes and the hometown of undefeated heavyweight world boxing champion Rocky Marciano, and the adopted hometown of world middleweight boxing champion Marvin Hagler.

Massasoit had a hockey team, even if not many people knew about it. And, as I started classes at Massasoit, good fortune struck in the person of Neil Higgins, who had played goalie at Boston College in the early 1970s. Neil recognized that I could play Division I, and he told me to consider Massasoit Community College to be my tryout for the big time. I could go through the motions at Massasoit, he said, and mope and play with a piss-poor attitude, or I could approach the opportunity as a proving point.

Well, I was a winning underdog. I used this to my advantage. Being overlooked and underappreciated kindled the flames. The Massasoit Warriors made it to the national community college championship game. I made 60 saves in that game, and we won 1-0. Word had been getting around about my play at Massasoit, and my performance in the championship game certified the talk that I could compete at the Division I level. Within a couple weeks, Boston University coach Jack Parker was at my family's home offering me a full scholarship.

Who would have thought that Massasoit Community College would be my opportunity to play big time college hockey?

You never know when that opportunity will present itself. When it does, you need to be ready and to commit and to go for it.

But as for that scholarship to BU—there was a complication.

"I already offered the scholarship to someone else," Coach Parker told me and my mom and dad.

What?

"But this kid has not made a decision," he continued. "And if he chooses to go someplace else, then the scholarship is yours."

"Well, who did you offer the scholarship to?" I asked.

"Mark Holden."

Holden was another Boston area goalie.

"Well, I've seen Holden play," I said. "And he is very good, but he is not as good as me."

Mark Holden ended up going to Brown University, but that decision was made only partly because of the opportunity of an Ivy League education. Another reason was that he thought he had a better chance of playing at Brown than he did at BU.

I got that scholarship.

When I showed up at BU, I wasn't readily embraced by the players on the team. Who could blame them? They were all recruited from strong hockey programs. I was recruited from Massasoit Community College, hardly a hockey hotbed.

I hadn't proven myself.

I was confident, though, that my chance was coming—and soon. And I would be ready.

Herb Brooks—A Winning Underdog for the Ages

There would have been no "Miracle on Ice" if Herb Brooks had not been cut from the 1960 U.S. Olympic hockey team. But he got cut, and in about the most painful way possible.

Only a couple weeks remained until the opening ceremonies of the Squaw Valley games, and Herb Brooks, a three-year starter for the Minnesota Golden Gophers, was on the team. He was even in the official team photo. Then U.S. coach Jack Riley received word from former Harvard University standout Bill Cleary that he was interested in playing for the U.S. squad—but only if his younger brother, Bob, who also starred at Harvard, was brought on as well. Riley, 37, who had grown up outside of Boston and had played hockey at Dartmouth College and was on the 1948 U.S. Olympic team, had wanted both the Cleary brothers to try out for the team, and if he could only have one of the brothers it would be Bill. But the Clearys were running an insurance business in Boston, and they couldn't leave the business for the two-month training camp and pre-Olympic game schedule. Two weeks, though, they could do. Riley felt he needed Bill Cleary to be competitive at Squaw Valley, and if that meant agreeing to the Bill and Bob package deal, then that is what he would do.

Room needed to be made for the Cleary brothers—and two players needed to be cut. One of those players was Bob Dupuis, a former All American at Boston University. The other player was Herb Brooks.

Herb didn't take it well—no surprise there. He got on the phone to his father, Herb Sr., who was back in Minnesota, and who had been critical of his son putting off getting a paying job so that he could chase Olympic glory, and started blabbering about how he had received a royal screwing.

"You aren't going to believe this dad; this is an East-West thing, and Riley had it in for me," Herb Jr. complained. "He needed some more Boston guys on this team, and I was the fall guy. This is so unfair; this is just out-and-out wrong . . . ."

The elder Brooks, a stern, no-nonsense insurance salesman, allowed his son to rant for a minute, and then said, "Are you done?"

Herb Jr. had no reply. His father, however, wasn't through talking.

"Because if you are finished explaining about how you got railroaded," continued Herb Sr., "then you take your playbook and you go see Coach Riley, and you shake his hand and thank him for giving you the chance. Next you shake the hand of every one of your former teammates and you wish them the best, and you tell them you hope for them that they win the gold. And then you get your butt on the next plane home to Minnesota."

It seems Herb Jr. should have sought a sympathetic ear elsewhere.

Herb Brooks made it back to Minnesota. Bill and Bob Cleary made it onto a U.S. team that entered the Olympics every bit like the underdog that would be the U.S. team that showed up 20 years later at Lake Placid.

Both Clearys were stellar at Squaw Valley, with Bill leading the team in scoring, and Bob third in scoring. The Americans had huge upsets over Canada and the Soviet Union on their way to a 6-0-0 record, and they qualified for the gold medal game against Czechoslovakia, also heavily favored against the Yanks.

It was February 27. Back at the Brooks family home in St. Paul, Herb Jr. and Sr. watched together the black and white telecast of the United States–Czechoslovakia game. The U.S. was behind, 4-3, after two periods. In the third period, the Americans scored six unanswered goals and won, 9-4.

My future coach watched the jubilation; he watched his former teammates celebrating, along with Bill and Bob Cleary. And still not a word of sympathy from his father. Herb Sr. did have words for his son, though. He turned to him and said, "Well, Herb, I guess they cut the right guy."

Those words kindled a competitive fire. They were akin to taking a flamethrower to a swimming pool full of gasoline.

Commit to Proving the Doubters Wrong

Well, Herb, I guess they cut the right guy. Ouch!

Herb Brooks always had a fiery spirit, and an outsized desire to compete and prove himself. It was February 1960 and the events of that month were the catalyst and the beginning, of something much more, much bigger. If Herb Brooks did not live that February 1960, there would not have been a U.S. hockey team standing atop the victory podium at Lake Placid in 1980.

Herb made the 1964 and 1968 U.S. Olympic teams, and he was a co-captain of each. Neither of those teams won medals. Herb realized an Olympic dream, but he also came close to being part of one of the greatest episodes not only in U.S. Olympic history, but in U.S. sports history. Coming so close and not making it would be the fuel and energy that supported his obsession to achieve something great, something epic, in hockey. Now, I am not so sure that in February 1960, or even in the few years following, that that achievement was specifically defined as coaching just the right team as it played optimum hockey on the world stage against the most talented competition yet assembled. Yet there is no doubt that that is what it became.

After his playing days, Herb became a coach, a great coach. He didn't need to have coached the 1980 U.S. team to achieve that distinction. At the helm of the University of Minnesota's Golden Gophers, he won three NCAA championships, in 1974, 1976, and 1979. Herb studied everyone and everything that had to do with hockey. He drove his players hard. He pulled greatness out of individuals, while never allowing for "one man" shows or prima donnas. In this way, he built a great program and great teams.

Herb was a winning underdog. Those athletes who played for him exemplified that trait, and so did his teams. Being a winning underdog and having something to prove is a powerful motivator; it focuses energy and the mind wonderfully.

For every member of the 1980 U.S. Olympic hockey team, every time we stepped on to the ice at Lake Placid to compete, we were winning underdogs committed to proving the doubters wrong.

Victor, Not Victim—Results, Not Reasons

Neil Higgins advised me not to mope. Herb Brooks moped when he got cut, and his father quickly and coldly let him know that there was no future in that.

When you are moping you are playing the victim, not the victor. You are looking for reasons to fail and are not delivering results.

Get ticked off. Get angry. Get focused. Get organized. Get smarter. Play the victor, not the victim. Results, not reasons.

Turn defeat and setback into positive energy, into the fuel and fire that nurtures success.

It's interesting—I am a big reader and lover of books. I also like to write. I write almost every day in a journal, and I handwrite at least 10 notes a week that I mail to people. I wrote the Foreword for the *New York Times* bestseller, *The Boys of Winter: The Untold Story of a Coach, a Dream, and the 1980 U.S. Olympic Hockey Team*, by Wayne Coffey; and now I am a co-author of the book you are now reading.

I bring all this up because among the best examples of people who are winning underdogs, who have something to prove, who stay after it, and who go on to achieve greatness, are writers.

History's most famous and accomplished writers used the rejection letters they received as a sort of motivation, even putting those letters in places where they were sure to confront them.

Jack London received more than 600 rejection letters before selling his first story; he framed and displayed some of the letters. Stephen King accumulated a large pile of rejection letters; he used to impale them on a spike to a wall in his home. F. Scott Fitzgerald wallpapered his bedroom with rejection letters. And on the topic of motivation, it seems that a young lady named Zelda Sayre, with whom F. Scott Fitzgerald was in big-time love, and to whom he proposed, said that, yes, she would marry him, but not before he published a novel.

Motivational speaker and bestselling author Joe Girard understands that rejection is just one step on the way to proving yourself. Mr. Girard says, "Every no gets you closer to yes."

Every no gets you closer to yes.

I like that.

■ ■ ■

When you are a winning underdog, you have something to prove and you prove it; you don't look for a way not to do something. You do it.

With best wishes to Jim Craig   *Jimmy Carter*

President Jimmy Carter, Jim, and First Lady Rosalynn Carter in the Oval Office, February 25, 1980.

Getting to the top of the podium at Lake Placid required the coaches and the players to repeatedly confront whether we were going to act like victims or victors. For most of us, that choice, and whether we had the fortitude to make the tough choice, resulted from upbringing and experiences that started early, when we were just kids. It started long before we all got together for the first time at the Olympic Training Center in Colorado Springs in the summer of 1979.

In recruiting and assembling the players for the 1980 team, Herb Brooks and assistant coach Craig Patrick evaluated and judged beyond the physical—beyond speed, passing, dexterity, strength, intelligence, and the capacity to build stamina (there is more about this in the "Picking the Right Players" chapter).

If you look at the makeup of the team, and go into the formative years of each player and each coach, you will discover a history rich with caring parents and supportive mentors. You will find virtues and strong community. What you won't find is a lot of money, luxury, indulgence, or downtime.

This upbringing was just the right clay and raw material from which could be molded and constructed a team that would work and sacrifice enough, would be tough enough, would have enough confidence, would not collapse under setback and defeat, which would have just enough respect for authority, and be just open and receptive enough to coaching and mentoring (while never sacrificing our edge and spirit), to take on the world and set a standard for overachievement.

When our coaches searched for the people who could win the unwinnable and beat the unbeatable, they found us. They found winning underdogs.

Expect Adversity—It Never Gets Easier

At Boston University, a few games into my sophomore year, I earned a starting position, alternating in the net with Brian Durocher. I went 20-5-1 that season, and we made it to the NCAA semifinals, losing to the University of Michigan.

It was a breakout season for me, and I was on the path to achieving my dreams. But then came more adversity—and this adversity hurt in a new and terrible way. My mother became seriously ill with cancer.

For a stretch of several weeks, she was an inpatient at Massachusetts General Hospital. Since it is located in Boston, I could travel to it on the trolley every day after practice to spend time with my mom. Almost every family gets hit with cancer, and it can be scary and very painful for both the patient and the people who love the patient. My mother was suffering, and I hurt. My mom knew that things didn't look good, and she knew she might not be around, in person that is, to see my biggest triumphs, in sport and in life. She did, though, want to be part of them, and she made me promise that if I ever had a chance to represent my country in hockey that I would do it, no matter the sacrifice. My mother also made me promise that I would graduate from college. I made those promises to her.

It was the following September and our entire family was down at a small cottage we owned on the south coast of Massachusetts, in a town called Mattapoisett, a few days prior to classes starting for my junior year. My mother was with us, spending her final days. Cancer had destroyed her; she weighed 46 lbs. I was swimming with my younger brothers at a beach about 300 yards from our cottage. I dove into the water, and as I descended into the cold and blackness, I was taken with a feeling of calm and understanding that my mom was gone; her suffering had been relieved. I got out of the water and told my brothers we were going back to the cottage. We had walked only a few steps, and I saw my older brother Don hurrying toward us. I knew what he was about to say.

I tell this story in my speeches, and a reason I share this with the audiences is that I feel that when someone who loves you dies, the spirit and energy of that person is passed to those people he or she loved. Perhaps that sounds very New Age to you, but I believe it. I also believe it is up to those who remain here on earth to take a hold of that spirit and energy and to do something positive and important with it. Making this commitment helps you to win no matter how much of an underdog you are—and no matter what you have to prove.

Accept the Challenge—Embrace the Opportunity

So I took that spirit and energy, and I got to work. In my junior year, I went 16-0-0 in goal, a record that included Boston University winning the ECAC and NCAA tournaments. In my senior year, I made All-American, and my play attracted the attention of Herb Brooks, who was coaching the U.S. squad that spring in the World Championships in Moscow.

He asked me if I wanted to be a part of the team, and I jumped at that chance. This would give me a good reason to skip class (with the understanding I would quickly go back and earn my degree), I would have a passport for the first time, and I could do some sightseeing.

But here's the thing—I wasn't heading overseas with something to prove. I felt at this time that I had kind of proven it. Sure, I had a dream to play in the Olympics, but now that Olympic-level competition was on my radar screen and directly ahead, well, I might have been lacking some enthusiasm. So, I was just going to travel, meet some foreign girls, sit on the bench with a towel around my neck (the posture of any good backup goalie), cheer on my teammates, and have one heck of time. I thought that Herb Brooks just needed me to fill out the roster.

Herb was actually thinking bigger picture for me. He had not yet been named as the coach of the 1980 Olympic hockey team, but he was in the running, and he was figuring in his head who his goalie would be for Lake Placid—and I was on his short list of three. Many top coaches and experts, though, felt that for the collegiate season that had just ended there were four or five better college goalies than Jim Craig. But Herb liked my confidence, my swagger. He understood that it was tough to overestimate the value of those traits when you are playing on the world stage. Little did Herb know that when I got on the plane to fly to the Soviet Union, I was a bit deficient in confidence and swagger.

In Moscow, the U.S. team lost its first game of the preliminary round to Canada, 6-3. It wasn't my fault; I didn't play. Up next was

Finland, and it was 1-1, late in the third period, and Herb Brooks looked down at the end of the bench—*toward where I was sitting*. I saw him looking for me—and I ducked. No, no, I wasn't on this trip to play. I was a passenger. I wanted to have no responsibility, and just have fun. Herb decided not to put me in. It was still 1-1 when the game ended.

We weren't going on to the medal round, but in two days we were playing the tournament's top seed, the Czechs, who were very much in contention for the gold medal and, because of the way the tournament points were tabulated to determine who won gold, silver, and bronze, the Czechs had every incentive to put a big whooping on the United States. This fact created all sorts of anxiety for me. You see, I was fairly certain that since we weren't going on to the medal round, and that our game against Czechoslovakia was our final game of the tournament, that Herb Brooks was going to start me in that game. I needed to dodge this bullet.

When the final horn sounded from the Finn game, I got to the locker room as fast as I could. I quickly threw off my uniform and got into my street clothes and started for the exit . . . and then . . . "Hey Jimmy."

Oh no.

It was Craig Patrick, our player coach, and the person whom Herb had picked to deliver me a message. I turned around to see Craig hurrying toward me.

"What's up?" I asked, nervously.

Craig had something of a mischievous smile, and he said, "Jimmy, I got some good news, and some bad news for you."

Okay, I decided to play along, and I asked first for the bad news, even if I was fairly certain I already knew what it was.

"Well, Jimmy, you are going to start against the Czechs. And we are going to get killed."

Yeah, that *was* bad news. *And the good news?*

Craig still had that smile; he said, "But you are going to learn a lot."

Oh, man I hadn't signed on for *this*.

I hadn't signed up to be the answer to any number of trivia questions, all of which were a variant of "In international ice hockey competition, which goalie let in the most goals in . . ." and here, take your pick, "the first minute of the game?" . . . one period?" . . . "two periods?" . . . "a game?"

I had to get out of this. Full of doubt and anxiety, I went back to the hotel and lay down on the bed and stared at the ceiling. I thought about all sorts of ways to render myself unavailable for the game. One option that was particularly attractive was to break my ankle. Sure, there would be physical pain, but it would save me from incalculable psychological injury.

After a while, though, I calmed and took stock of things. I needed to take on and embrace the challenge. I wanted to play in the Olympics. How the heck could I ever play in the Olympics if I couldn't summon the fortitude to play in the World Championships? I resolved that I was going to be in net against Czechoslovakia.

I didn't sleep well that night, but practice the next day was a great way to expend nervous energy. The night prior to the game, I tossed and turned. But on Tuesday, April 17, I made it to the Palace of Sports at the Central Lenin Stadium. It was show time. I remember those warm-ups, skating the ice. I was so nervous and my mouth and throat were so dry that I couldn't even swallow. Seriously, I tried to take a drink of water, and it wouldn't go down.

The game started, and I was still a bit frozen with fear; I wasn't moving that well. After maybe 30 seconds into the game, I faced the first shot. I did nothing to prevent it, and I had not reacted to the puck when it came. I am eternally grateful that the puck hit me, because if it hadn't, I think my competitive hockey career would have ended that day. But the puck did hit me; it came on a slap shot, and I was literally slapped out of my "deer in the headlights" stupor. I got down to doing what I worked so hard to do for so many years.

I backed my teammates up; I played my game. My confidence returned—and so did my swagger. I made 59 saves, and we raised a whole lot of eyebrows when we tied the Czechs, 2-2.

That was the game in which Herb Brooks decided that if he coached the U.S. team at Lake Placid then I would be his goaltender.

Beyond the Ice—Other Coaches and Mentors

Sentinel Investments, a company for which I have delivered three keynote addresses, competes with a winning underdog attitude. It is an attitude, a mindset, which underpins its success. Established in 1934, and based in Montpelier, Vermont, Sentinel is an award winning mutual funds firm. It employs approximately 130 people in five offices across the United States.

Midway through 2010, Sentinel had more than $18 billion under management. That is a lot of money, but even that figure wouldn't put it in the top 100 companies in terms of assets under management. Consider that industry leaders in that category, such as Vanguard Group, Fidelity, and American Funds, each manage more than $1 trillion (with a trillion equal to 1000 billions). You aren't a top-10 player unless you are managing in the neighborhood of $150 billion.

But Sentinel Investments understands and is fully confident in the value it offers investors. Indeed, its products have long been a choice of investors and investment managers and advisers looking for funds that outperform, in a down market, the bigger and better known funds. Its products are known as "value funds"—not high risk or having a big potential for fast and stratospheric growth, but more conservative investments, with a consistent track record of stability and positive returns.

Sentinel Investments has its place—an important and essential place—and the company wants everyone to know it. One of its primary marketing messages is "Mere size and 'being all things to all people' do not concern us. We measure success by our ability to withstand the tests of time, as a provider of core 'back to basics' strategies."

When a manager or adviser is planning and putting together an investment strategy and portfolio for a client—when he is figuring on the best way to protect and grow the client's money—Sentinel wants its funds to be in the mix. Jim Cronin, president of Sentinel Investments, even embraces the "little guy" identity of the company, and leverages that identity to position it on the radar screen of the organizations entrusted to invest and manage the hard-earned dollars of Americans. When presenting at a meeting, he is fond of saying, with a coy smile, that "Sentinel Investments *is* the largest money management firm in Vermont."

Two of the keynotes I delivered for Sentinel were a few weeks apart, in May 2009, in Stamford, Connecticut. The speeches were a component of a Sentinel Investments effort to capitalize on the impending Morgan Stanley purchase of Smith Barney, the money management division of Citigroup, an epic merger that would create the firm Morgan Stanley Smith Barney. The merger was finalized in June 2009, with Morgan Stanley owning 51 percent and controlling interest in the new concern.

As the two firms prepared to ink the deal, the top producers from Morgan Stanley and Smith Barney were, of course, offered strong financial incentives to get on board with the venture. As well, these all-star managers and advisers were brought in to meetings so that they could be pitched and recruited in a more targeted and personalized fashion.

Sentinel Investments recognized that these meetings offered an exceptional opportunity—a place where everyone in the room was either a client with which it needed to solidify and strengthen a relationship, or a potential client. Two of the meetings were set for Stamford. And the managers and advisers invited to these meetings were the crème de la crème, those who, on the low end, managed a few million dollars, and who, on the high end, managed $100 million or more.

Big money. Big opportunity. And Sentinel—yes, *that* Sentinel, the largest money management firm in Vermont—decided it would sponsor dinners at the Stamford meetings, and bring me in to deliver keynotes. Sentinel had that energy; it always has that energy; it has something to prove.

Sentinel said it wanted an inspiring and entertaining speech, one that included interesting anecdotes from my experience in preparing for and playing in the Olympics. Sentinel also made sure that I talked with the Morgan Stanley and Smith Barney managers at the meeting so that I could hit the right words and themes, and speak to their objectives.

Jim Cronin spoke prior to my appearance in Stamford, and he included the "largest money management firm in Vermont" line. He introduced me. I talked for about 45 minutes and took questions. Sentinel also had other senior management attending the event, so they could meet with Morgan Stanley and Smith Barney people and talk more about the value that Sentinel offers.

One of those senior managers on site was Clara Sierra, executive vice president of Sentinel. Smart and always upbeat, smiling, engaged, and personable, Clara is the embodiment of a company that has something to prove, and is doing something about it.

"We are motivated day after day, in competing against companies that are much bigger than us," said Clara. "We are a confident underdog, an underdog that understands it has what it takes to beat bigger and better known firms. We get after it and go head to head against the favorites; we do so with enthusiasm and confidence."

Clara works out of the Sentinel's New York City office. So she is on the ground playing with the big boys—and Clara is a lady that does not take a backseat to any of them, and neither does the company for which she works. Clara said that Sentinel Investments doesn't use the down economy as an excuse to not compete and to not set ambitious goals.

"Especially in recession, it would be easy for Sentinel Investments to play the 'woe is me' card—but we don't do that," said Clara. "Sure, we see the recession for what it is—a big hill to climb, an obstacle. But we also see it as a major opportunity. Sentinel may be smaller than the competition, but we look at it as an asset, helping us to be nimbler and more responsive and better able to adapt, all qualities that are more important when the economy is hurting than when it is healthy and strong."

I'm encouraged and happy to report that things are going well for Sentinel Investments. Among the good news—on March 24, 2010, the *Sentinel Government Securities Fund, Class A* won the 2010 Lipper Fund Award for "Best U.S. General Government Fund over 10 Years."

Great Teams Think of Themselves as Winning Underdogs—Chapter Recap

- **Kindle Your Competitive Fire:** Get in touch and hold tight to what drives you and what motivates you. Focus on it. Let it feed the flames of your desire to succeed.
- **Commit to Proving the Doubters Wrong:** Recognize that the world is full of experts who have been proven wrong. If you want to find someone to doubt you, or locate a cynic, the search won't take long nor be difficult. Believe in yourself—even if you are the only one who believes in you.
- **Victor, Not Victim—Results, Not Reasons:** No excuses— just get it done.
- **Expect Adversity—It Never Gets Easier:** You have worked hard and sacrificed and overcome many obstacles. You have earned success and no more barriers should be thrown your way. Right? It wouldn't be fair now to face more adversity. Right? Well, life isn't fair. When you overcome one obstacle, get ready for the next.
- **Accept the Challenge—Embrace the Opportunity:** Be more than a practice player. Training, sacrificing, and dreaming without giving it all in the arena is not the character of a champion.

2

Great Teams Have a Shared Dream

Real unselfishness consists in sharing the interests of others.

—GEORGE SANTAYANA

A merica is the greatest nation on earth. I believe that fully. We aren't perfect and we've made a lot of mistakes; we've committed our sins. But there is no country that does a better job of protecting our God-given rights. No place provides more opportunity than the United States. We were founded on a good idea—actually a lot of good ideas—and if we can keep true to them we will maintain the greatness and qualities that make us exceptional.

We are the greatest nation on earth because we are the best at taking the strengths and positive values of people from so many ethnic and racial and cultural and religious backgrounds and getting these people to share a dream.

Members of great teams have a shared dream.

Growing up we read and heard our country described as "The Melting Pot" and "A Nation of Nations" and a "Nation of Immigrants." How we bring people together and get people working together and stay focused on the same goal is one of the most important components of our greatness.

E Pluribus Unum—Latin for "Out of Many, One"—is our national motto.

E Pluribus Unum could also be a motto for any organization or team that hopes to win and achieve something enduring and extraordinary.

E Pluribus Unum is also about having a shared dream.

When America is at its best, it is a family and a community with a common identity, values, laws—and hopefully objectives. We don't stay great—we don't hold tightly to that shared dream—without family and without community.

I am concerned, though, that both institutions are imperiled.

Building and keeping a family and community together requires—and I state this over and over—lots of hard and smart work. This should be a consolation, not something that discourages you. Greatness and making history are not achieved without hours and hours, and then more hours and hours, of hard and smart work.

With few exceptions, among them family and community, I think that things in society are better today than yesterday, and not as good as they will be tomorrow. You hear that term, "The Good Old Days," and it sounds like we left the best of times behind, that everything is breaking and falling down, and that it will never get built back up. Well, for the most part, and just ask people that are older than you, the good old days were not nearly as good as today.

Family and community were stronger yesterday, though. You can have all the money and technology and convenience possible, but a happy and healthy society still needs strong families and strong community. This is when society is at its best. Family and community are tightly connected—one is an extension of and supports the other. The network of friends and families and neighbors who share values, who socialize together, who help one another, and who share common dreams and objectives is so important. The concepts of family and community are vital to the success of winning teams and winning organizations.

Is your organization a family? Is it a community? What type of family and community have you fostered? Is there more that divides your employees than unites them? Do your people trust one another? Can they rely on one another? Where has your group been? Where is it going? How hard and closely will your people work together to get there? What are your values?

Who are you?

What are you?

■ ■ ■

For close to 25 years, I worked for companies. Then in 2006 I launched my own company, Gold Medal Strategies (GMS). Prior to starting my own enterprise, I worked for some wonderful people; they mentored me and made me a better professional and a better person. Still, I must tell you that my experience in corporate America impressed upon me that few divisions, companies, or enterprises operated with a common purpose and a common goal.

Too many employees were not playing team, and were far too focused on themselves. And this conduct could continue because companies could get along and make money—and people could continue to make their mortgage and car payments, contribute to their 401(k)s, and save for their kids' college educations—without playing as a team and working toward achieving something great, together.

This is why the experience of the 1980 U.S. Olympic hockey team is so valuable. We could not have achieved greatness if we were selfish individuals and if we didn't keep an eye on the bigger prize. We could not have won the game that couldn't be won, or beat the team that couldn't be beat, unless we bought into a common objective and prepared and competed in unison to achieve that objective.

We had a shared dream.

In July 1979, 64 of the top amateur hockey players in America—among them the 20 players who would make up the team that showed up at Lake Placid—were in Colorado Springs at the Olympic Training Center to compete in a tournament at the U.S. Sports Festival. This tournament was the final opportunity for a player to make a case that he should be on the Olympic squad.

Almost to a man, the end game for those at Colorado Springs was to make it to the NHL. This Olympic business, while important and prestigious, was mostly a stepping-stone. We would spend some time together, all the while holding tight to our own individual dreams. When the Olympics were over, and we departed from Lake Placid without a medal but some fun experiences, we would make our try for the pros.

We weren't a real team and we did not share a dream. There was considerable dissension among us. Even beyond the fact that players were competing against each other for spots on the team, there were also regional rivalries (primarily described as East versus West, or Boston versus Minnesota). If you want some visual shorthand for the heft these rivalries and divisions carried, watch the scene in the movie *Miracle* in which my character, played by Eddie Cahill, is looking over a preliminary U.S. team roster that is on the wall. Jack O'Callahan, played by Peter Horton, comes along, calls me a "sieve," and asks how the roster is looking. I smile and say, "A lot of guys from Minnesota and Boston." O'Callahan smirks and responds, "Yeah, like that's gonna work."

Hollywood did an accurate job of portraying the potential for the Minnesota and Boston guys to work well together. It was going to be tough.

We thought the Midwest guys were all farm boys and backwoods types, all lacking savvy about the real world. They thought we were wise guys, slick urban kids.

I'll give you a good inside story on the coming together of separate cultures and how trust and acceptance can be an issue. Our team was just about set; it was late summer of 1979. Assigned adjoining lockers were Rob McClanahan, a country kid from Minnesota, and Jack O'Callahan, my teammate from Boston University, who grew up in the Boston neighborhood of Charlestown, which was largely a mix of Irish and Italians. Rob grew up on a farm where the outdoors seemed to go on forever. Jack—whom we called "OC"—grew up in a triple-decker that was bordered on the left by a triple-decker and on the right by a triple-decker with about only 10 feet separating one building from the other. Rob had cows for neighbors. Jack had the most interesting and curious mix of neighbors—cops, firemen, postal workers, bureaucrats, priests, nuns, shopkeepers, and many colorful characters whose jobs were, let's say, "off the books."

Rob was getting ready for practice; he took off his street clothes and then looked at the tough Boston guy standing next to him—the one, by the way, who had a scar along his cheek. Rob suddenly became very concerned about his wallet. He deftly shoved it in his shoe and placed it under his shirt in the locker.

I could have told Rob that he had nothing to worry about from OC, who is as stand-up and honest as the day is long, but prejudices and preconceptions take a while to dispel.

We had to work hard to get through the rivalries and distrust and cynicism that undermined us coming together. The process was not smooth and it was often painful. Emotions got heated and there was shouting and even some physical scraps. But we did come together. We became one of the best examples, ever, of members of a team operating cohesively, in synch, and cooperatively in pursuit of a common goal.

In this chapter, I describe how we grew together to share a dream and what elements are important in this process.

Make the Quest Epic

If you want your employees to share a dream, then establish a goal for them that is almost beyond their reach—that is maybe beyond their reach. Tell them that they have been charged with doing something epic.

Often when I speak to a group, near the end of my speech I will tell them that I plan to return to speak to it again, and that prior to me returning, I want the group to have accomplished a major goal—or to hold a higher and more established position in its industry than the one it now holds. That might mean moving from 20th to 10th place among the biggest companies in its field. Or it might mean holding 5th place far more securely than it now does—putting more distance between itself and 6th place, and perhaps moving on the shoulder of 4th place. Maybe it means that instead of scoring the silver medal it now stands atop the victory platform.

For each group, an epic quest means something different.

■ ■ ■

Early on, the 1980 U.S. Olympic hockey team had an epic quest—a Quixotic and maybe unreachable goal. Let's forget about the preposterous notion of winning a gold medal. That is not the quest I am talking about. In fact, such was the nature of the quest that coaching or playing for the 1980 U.S. Olympic hockey team was not a popular or highly-sought gig. The Yanks had not done well in recent international hockey competition, and there was little to suggest that fortunes would change. Why sign on to something and work your tail off and sacrifice for six months, only to get trounced on the world stage? Especially if you could forego all of that and sign an NHL contract and make some money.

What the players didn't know, but what assistant coach Craig Patrick was aware of, was that while Herb Brooks may have talked openly about a bronze medal being the highest prize we could hope to win, the quest that moved and motivated him was a medal of a different color.

The good thing, of course, about an epic quest or an Impossible Dream or Shooting for the Stars, or whatever you call it, is that those who take up the cause in pursuit of the goal are especially motivated and driven. That is why there is value in laying it on the line in terms of just how difficult, strenuous, and obstacle-laden will be the course to reach the goal. If you downplay what is necessary to achieve the goal, then you aren't going to have the quality and passion on board to win.

Great challenges and daunting missions invite rare souls, strong characters, and indomitable wills. These challenges and missions inspire and bring about achievement beyond the imagined.

My teammates and I were constantly challenged. In the early stages, as we came together, there was next to no talk about any gold medal. But we had impressed upon us from the get-go that the 1980 team had been commissioned to accomplish the following two seemingly unachievable tasks which, whether we had figured it out yet, would put us in play to do something very special:

1. Be the best-conditioned hockey team competing at Lake Placid.

2. Play, with exceptional precision, a revolutionary form of hockey that combined the bruising, dump and chase game of the Americans and Canadians with the elegant, frequent, and precise passing of the Eastern Europeans and Soviets.

Herb Brooks told us we would be fresher and have stronger legs in the third period than would the Soviets, and that we would play *our* game while at the same time throwing *their* game back at them. He was crazy.

Then again, as he told us often, "You can't be common; the common man goes nowhere. You have to be uncommon."

The road to uncommon and the impossible would be one on which we would have to train and punish ourselves like no other team had in U.S. hockey history. Things were going to change.

As things had been done in the past, about a month prior to the Olympics, the best amateur hockey players in America showed up in Boston and Minneapolis, and the powers that be selected a squad. The players received nice blue blazers and, maybe, a cardigan with an official patch on the sleeve. The team did a quick barnstorm of America, raising money for U.S.A. Hockey, the group governing amateur hockey in America, and then played games against college and minor league teams it knew it could beat. It was then off to the Olympics to quickly lose two games and not make the medal round.

Our team assembled six months prior to the Olympics. Then we got to work. Man, we trained harder than we could have imagined. Skating, skating, and more skating. Weightlifting. Plyometrics. Drill after drill after drill. Chalk talks and team meetings and watching miles of videotape, scrutinizing every pass and every movement of every player on every team we would or might compete against at Lake Placid.

Over about a five-month stretch, starting in early September and finishing up in early February, a few days prior to the start of the Olympics, we played 61 games, oftentimes practicing on the same day of a game. We played top college and amateur teams, and faced off against NHL squads. We toured Europe and played various national teams. We played a holiday tournament in Lake Placid and beat a very good Soviet "B" team.

As we sacrificed and worked so hard, we felt it was worth it because more and more, day after day, we recognized we were on an epic quest. We were being conditioned and prepared to upend history and confound convention.

We were 20 men sharing one dream—no matter how seemingly impossible or foolish that dream may have seemed to everyone but ourselves.

Together on the podium, *all 20 players*. The podium celebration is Jim's favorite memory of the Olympics.

Credit: Photographer: Focus on Sport/Getty Images

Have a Clearly Defined Mission, Values, and Messages

I have a saying that I repeat over and over when coaching and advising companies: "If you don't know where you are going, any path will get you there."

It is amazing how many companies and other organizations don't know where they are going and their employees are wandering along their own paths—not the same path. Some of the most successful companies have even managed to lose focus and stray.

■ ■ ■

I enjoy moderating, steering discussion, and idea generation at executive and management roundtables. Maybe it is because I come from a big family and there is a bit of subconscious longing for my old dinner table and its spirited gab, laughter, and storytelling.

Combine that with my affection for helping to build consensus, and the fulfillment I receive from challenging, questioning, and coaching; therein is why I like this particular paradigm so much.

Roundtables can be a figurative and literal spoke of an organizational wheel that produces a shared dream. It is here where you can bang out and argue the mission, values, and primary messages for your company.

I advise groups to make sure that the objective of the roundtable is clearly defined prior to the meeting (remarkably this is not always the case). I suggest that when planning and coordinating a roundtable, homework should be assigned to the participants beforehand. Pick a book or a movie or a magazine article—or any combination thereof—that will facilitate and engender thought and which will get the creative juices flowing. Maybe assign the reading of a corporate case study—or the study of a public policy decision or debate.

When you assign the homework, tell the participants that the book or movie, or whatever the assignment is, will be a sort of locus for talking, generating ideas, and for helping to find agreement—as well as to name and describe a shared dream.

Companies that have hired me to speak have sent copies of the Disney movie *Miracle* to meeting attendees prior to the event, along with a list of teamwork teaching points that can be found in the film. This teamwork-building tactic has received strong approval and reviews.

Ira Riklis, the president and founder of Sutherland Capital, the nation's largest owner and operator of alarm and alarm-monitoring companies, gave his senior management team copies of *Miracle* following an off-site meeting in which I participated. Ira advised the team members to watch the film to reacquaint themselves with the elements of teamwork discussed during the roundtable and retreat.

I have presided over three roundtables for Sutherland Capital. Ira is a highly intelligent, creative businessman, and a philanthropist with many interests. When he plans an executive powwow he thinks it over and does it up right.

In May 2010, I sat down with his leadership team at a beautiful lodge in a village I know well: Lake Placid, New York.

Ira assigned me preparatory homework. He asked me to watch the 1952 film, *The Bad and the Beautiful,* directed by Vincente Minnelli, and starring Lana Turner, Kirk Douglas, Walter Pidgeon, and Gloria Grahame. *The Bad and the Beautiful*, which won five Academy Awards, tells the story of the rise and fall of a movie producer named Jonathan Shields. Through flashbacks, we learn how on his way to the top he helped out, but also hurt, an actress, a director, and a writer. Now Shields needs a break to revive his career and goes back to the three, all of whom are successful, for help. They refuse. But as the movie ends we can see how each of them is torn and, perhaps, willing to take on torment again to reach even higher in Hollywood.

Ira's execs didn't watch the film together until the morning of the day of our get together; the start of our roundtable would be early afternoon.

Following the movie, with *The Bad and the Beautiful* story still fresh and moving in everyone's minds, I established a discussion that intertwined and connected where Sutherland Capital was positioned in the marketplace, what was necessary to improve on its position of industry leadership, and what personally would be required from each member of management. We dug deep, all of us, into issues of responsibility to the company, to one's self, to one's family, and to society. What was worth it to sacrifice? What went too far? Ira and his team were happy with what we found out and what we decided.

Jim addresses members of Sutherland Capital management during an appearance at the Herb Brooks Arena in Lake Placid in the same locker room that Jim and his teammates used for their game against the Soviet Union.
Credit: Jackie Kelly, Olympic Regional Development Authority

"As usual, at our Lake Placid retreat, Jim led and directed and held a mirror to the face of Sutherland management," said Ira. "He helped us be honest with ourselves, and he inspired us to be open and honest in our talk about who we are and where we need to go. Jim enticed spirited discussion about our values. When we left Lake

Placid, we were all far more in synch, far more on the same page than when we arrived."

Of my efforts to help players share a dream, this is the type of review I like to receive.

Get the mission and get the values right. Get agreement. Because if you don't, then you don't know where you are going; the path you are on will take you someplace—just not the place you need to go.

Get with the Program—Or Get Out

Perhaps you might find the title of this section a bit harsh. Well, anyone who has known me for a while can tell you that I am nothing if not forthright. I have toned it down a little bit through the years, but not too much.

If you want to win, people within your organization need to get with the program, be on board, support the effort—or they need to go someplace else. You can have the smartest and hardest working and most focused employee in the universe, but if that person doesn't agree and support the plan, then you have negative energy in your midst. You can talk with this person and see if there is a desire to get with the program, but if it isn't there then I suggest your decision is a fairly easy one. You are doing your group, and the person, a favor by moving him or her toward the door. Some of the most successful business people didn't mesh with the culture of one organization but signed with another and had success—sometimes tremendous success.

Of course, one type for which you should have little to no toleration is the cynic and the bad attitude. Troublemakers can sometimes be an asset—but cynics and bad attitudes just sap the strength of an organization. If you want to be a great team, then you need everyone to get onboard. If they won't get onboard then they need to . . . well . . . you know.

■ ■ ■

The dynamic of team sports demonstrates, as clearly as any, the importance of every group member being on board and with the program. Even the biggest winners and solid team players, those with a long and deep track record of being on top and being there for teammates, sometimes even they don't buy-in, or they develop a problem with organizational direction, or they cop an attitude. Be aware of this potential. Learn to recognize and deal with it.

Back in the fall of 2004, I had an opportunity to impart words of advice to a big-time winner, one who I thought might be copping a bit of an attitude—and that attitude might just undermine and throw off track one of the most magnificent comebacks in sports history. I couldn't let that happen, especially when the team on the comeback was my beloved Boston Red Sox.

In the 2004 American League Championship Series, the perennial nemesis of the Boston Red Sox—yes, those damn Yankees—went up three games to zip against the Sox. It looked dismal for Boston. Heck, in the third game of the series, the Yankees beat the Red Sox, 19-8, at Fenway Park. Any hope of a Boston comeback was about as far-fetched as the 1980 U.S. Olympic hockey team beating the Soviets at Lake Placid. It wasn't going to happen.

The Sox were up against it, and Boston general manager Theo Epstein figured that some miracle karma was needed to keep the season alive. He called me and asked if I would throw out the ceremonial first pitch for Game 4. Would I? Man, what a thrill. I had a conflict, though. I was scheduled in Las Vegas for a speech the same night of the game. I regretfully told Theo that I couldn't do it.

Lo and behold, the Sox didn't need me to send any miracle magic their way. They won in extra innings. (There is a lot to talk about in the game, but just think of a Dave Roberts steal in the ninth inning, and a David "Big Papi" Ortiz home run swing in the twelfth.) Boston won game five, again from a Big Papi walk-off RBI. The series went back to the Bronx and, well, you know where this was going. Game six was a BoSox win, setting up one of the most anticipated sports events ever.

All the marbles—a trip to the World Series—hinged on the seventh game at Yankee Stadium. I was back in the Boston area the night of the game, driving my car; my son JD was with me. It was about seven o'clock. My mobile phone rang and JD answered it. JD said hello, and then said, "No, this is his son, JD; he's right here." JD handed the phone to me, saying, "Dad, it's Theo Epstein; he asked for you."

Theo Epstein? Didn't he have more important things to do that night than to chat with me?

I got on the phone and came to find out, as Theo told me, that the Red Sox had been watching the movie *Miracle* in the clubhouse at Yankee Stadium. Theo had been pushing that Olympic hockey magic—and the concept of a shared dream—all along. Theo said he was going to put Derek Lowe, the Sox starting pitcher for the game, on the phone. He wanted me to give him some words of advice. I actually had a little bit in common with Derek, and when he got on the phone I told him this. In his most recent start against the Yankees, he had been shellacked. When I took to the ice in the Olympics against the Soviet Union, my previous outing against the Big Bad Red Machine had not gone well; we had been trounced, 10-3, at Madison Square Garden.

I knew that Derek Lowe was probably consumed with the task ahead, so I provided an elevator pitch-style pick-me-up and stream of advice. I mentioned to him that I knew that when the season ended he would be a free agent and in position to make even more serious money than he was presently making. I also said that I thought that he had been doing a bit of pissing and moaning on the field as of late, and that attitude could not serve anyone well, especially later that night. If a teammate wasn't doing well, it was hurting the team first, Derek Lowe second. I told Derek to just do his job, and not to think of getting through an entire game, but rather one inning at a time. I hoped this contributed to the shared dream mentality that would be needed to complete the comeback.

I don't know if my advice did any good; I do know that Lowe pitched one-hit ball for seven innings, and he remained focused on pitching and fielding and getting outs. The Sox won easily, a big and necessary step on the road to their first World Series title in 86 years.

Leverage Individuality for Team Strength

When building an organization whose people share a dream, don't destroy individual identity and discourage personal initiative. Leverage and capitalize on both.

Herb Brooks had a saying—"I don't believe in making many rules because the best players break them." There are many ways to take this comment. I take it as a combination of "you have to have common sense in rule and law making" and "everyone is different and you need to provide some individual wiggle room."

Vince Lombardi was a tough disciplinarian but he was also known for giving a bit of that wiggle room to his Green Bay Packers players. One of those players was the fun-loving wide receiver Max McGee, a notorious playboy. McGee was not known as a football player—curiously enough—who was keen on contact, and he didn't particularly like the tackling and blocking drills, which would involve players lining up and one after another tackling a ball carrier or blocking a tackler. You moved through the line, you had your turn, and then went to the back of the line. Somehow, Max McGee never made it to the front of the line. And Vince Lombardi, who didn't miss anything, didn't seem to notice.

On the 1980 team we let individuality—and even regionalism—work for us. I'll explain.

Three of my teammates—William "Buzzy" Schneider, Mark "Pav" Pavelich, and John "Bah" Harrington—came from the northeast section of Minnesota called the Iron Range. It was called the Iron Range because it was the mining of iron ore that largely supported people in the region—until the supply was mined-out and foreign countries could dig and extract and pull up the ore more cheaply.

You had to be tough and self-reliant to live in the Iron Range, a place with a lot of beauty, with forests and lakes and hills, yet where almost no one made a lot of money, where temperatures in the winter would get as low as 40 below zero Fahrenheit, and where total snowfall of more than 100 inches for the season was not uncommon.

The guys from "The Range" were tough and hardened and, as Wayne Coffey noted in *The Boys of Winter*, "They had their own style of hockey—intuitive and organic and grinding—on The Range, and their own way of life, too. Before PlayStations and play dates and ultra-organized youth hockey, there was hunting season and fishing season and hockey season."

Buzzy, Pav, and Bah shared a culture, an upbringing, and a way of playing hockey. Herb saw this and chose to work with it. He put all three on the same line—a line called the Conehead Line, a name inspired by the alien characters on the TV show *Saturday Night Live*.

"They were the only line that stayed intact because no one could play with them," said Mike Eruzione in an ESPN interview. "I played with them once, and I had no idea what I was doing or where I was going."

Iron Range Hockey was creative and explosive and unpredictable. And it gave our opponents a heavy dose of trouble.

Bring People Together—In One Place

I do 50 to 60 appearances a year, with those appearances being a mix of keynote addresses, spokesperson work, teamwork coaching, steering and moderating executive roundtables, meet and greets, and signings.

I have clients with whom I have worked for several years. Some organizations I work with design an engagement with one primary objective that may roll out over a few months or even up to a year or more, and may involve me delivering motivational addresses, providing teamwork coaching, and taping audio and video messages that are delivered online to employees and associates. What is often part of the engagement, whether it is a one-off or multi-event, are customized items I sign that are created to leverage and keep vibrant important messages and lessons. For example, a 4″ × 6″ card with an image of me wrapped in the American flag on one side, which I sign; the other side may be printed with a company logo and the theme of a meeting at which I spoke, or maybe a list of primary messages that management wants to remain front and center in the minds of employees.

Getting everyone on board and committed to a common goal—just like everything else in effective teamwork building— requires a lot of smart and hard work. I know, I know, I use that phrase over and over—and I do it for a reason.

Meetings, "off-sites," and retreats are helpful in building and as-sembling a team of people sharing a dream. Even in the day of the Internet and a variety of instantaneous digital communication—and let's not forget the phone, still the most effective interactive technology—people still need to get together in the same room. Again, team sports are valuable in teaching traits and qualities that can help companies win. In order to be successful, you have to get on the ice, the field, or the court, and you need to work hard and hurt together, communicate, get in synch, and support one another.

When players on a team are preparing to take to the field or ice or court, they get into the locker room and they take off their individual clothes—their "street" clothes—and they don the same uniform. They leave their iPods and cell phones in their lockers. The video games, computers, and flat screen TVs are at home.

When the ball goes up and the puck is dropped, you communicate the old fashioned way—by talking, hand gestures, a nod of the head, and a zillion other methods that were in vogue a couple hundred years ago and still are today.

True teamwork is not created with a text message or an e-mail. Videoconferencing and web conferencing allow organizations to get people together in one space virtually—and I have delivered speeches and coaching through both mediums and platforms—but it is still not an optimum experience. As I've already described, fundamental to the success of the 1980 U.S. Olympic hockey team was the length of time we spent together. The value of that time together was not just practice, conditioning, and game time, but also socializing, getting to know one another better, and learning to trust one another.

When the Boston and Minnesota guys sat down for a beer and pizza and got talking and built camaraderie *off* the ice, it all helped our efficiency *on* the ice. Victory at Lake Placid had a whole lot to do with the fact that we were a family.

Victory at Lake Placid was prepared for and earned during breakout drills, up-and-backs, team runs, watching film, and playing against tough competition. It was also prepared for and earned during the long train and bus rides we took together, and lugging our equipment, suitcases, and hockey bags together. As we shared stories about things other than hockey, as we grew to understand that we were all now one team, and not a collection of guys who played for different universities and who came from different places, we were making possible the magic and improbability that played out in February 1980 in the Adirondacks.

As you build, coach, and mentor your team, remember that their ability to win sales or produce the highest quality product can be greatly enhanced outside of the office or any conference or boardroom. Cultivating camaraderie, forging strong teamwork and strong teams, can be done in many different ways and can take many different forms.

Your employees need to know each other as people—as fathers and mothers, sisters and brothers, as those with hopes for their families and for themselves, as those with fears and dislikes, those with hobbies and loves, those with triumphs and losses, those with anguish and great joys, those with strengths and weaknesses. You learn and grow in this understanding when you get together for business and for socializing and friendship. All of it wins games and brings victories.

A story told about the 1980 team coming together involves Bill Baker's twenty-third birthday party—a few days after Thanksgiving

1979. Since July and Colorado, so much regionalism had dissolved, so much dissension had been eliminated, and so much trust had been formed. We were a family. Bill's birthday party wonderfully demonstrated this. In their book, *One Goal: A Chronicle of the 1980 U.S. Olympic Hockey Team,* John Powers and Arthur C. Kaminsky provide an inside look at the bash in which pheasant (supplied by Bill) was on the menu:

> . . . the function room at the Burnsville apartment complex had been reserved. Baker had done up the pheasants; Gayle Schneider, Buzzy's wife, had fixed a turkey. There was wild rice, birthday cake, a punch concocted by Jack O'Callahan and Jack Hughes, and only a dozen more beers than necessary.
>
> Around one in the morning, the soiree began unraveling. Mark Pavelich, who normally wouldn't say boo to a goose, began flinging pheasant bones. Cake began adorning the walls. Then Bobby Suter, who had his freshly broken ankle in a cast and was looking for a release valve, began pouring beer onto Mike Eruzione; Pavelich joined him.

Things got messy—but everyone had a blast. It was the type of fun and revelry that we could not have had even two months prior. And it was a party that helped bring us together and make us better on the ice.

My career is largely one of speaking to and coaching people in one place. Organizations with which I work not only bring in speakers, but they also hire teamwork facilitators and coaches. Depending on the event, I may provide both services. There are also groups that companies hire to run fun and challenging team-building drills and exercises. All these services, if used wisely and strategically, can provide immense help in putting together a winning team.

When planning these company get-togethers it is essential that comprehensive preparation is done to insure that the experience and opportunity is not wasted. If you are working with a speaker and other teamwork-building vendors, you need to have an open and thorough dialogue that brings everyone involved in the event together so that that all messages and objectives are the same for everyone and everyone is working toward the same goal.

■ ■ ■

For every engagement I do, GMS holds a conference call with the client—and prior to the call the client sends us its background information—and Gold Medal Strategies does its own research on the client as well. We prepare to prepare. Indeed, a favorite maxim of mine is "If you fail to prepare, you are preparing to fail."

During the conference call, my staff and I listen intently and ask the probing questions, all of which serve the purpose of understanding the organization better and precisely what needs to be achieved through the speech or seminar I will deliver. We discuss the objective of the event, its theme, the mission and values of the company, where it has been and where it is going, what are its strengths, its weaknesses, its primary competition, its challenges . . . and so much more. If GMS doesn't do this prep work then my client does not receive premium value and a competitive advantage from its investment in me.

It is tremendously heartening and encouraging seeing how much positive feedback GMS receives from clients *prior* to the event. GMS intends to be an excellent organization with which to work, from start to finish—from pre-planning to follow-up and beyond.

And I never forget that I am the president of GMS—and if I can't manage and run my own company with success, why would anyone hire me to advise and coach theirs?

Beyond the Ice—Other Mentors and Coaches

In the late 1980s, journalist Bill Moyers interviewed Peter Drucker, the father of modern business management theory. Drucker weighed in on the importance of making the quest epic and setting high standards, recalling an announcement President Franklin D. Roosevelt made early in World War II.

> I will never forget when Roosevelt announced that we would build thirty thousand fighter planes. I was on the task force that worked on our economic strength, and we had just reached the conclusion that we could build, at most, four thousand. We thought, "For goodness sake—he's senile!" Two years later we built fifty thousand. I don't know whether he knew, or if he just realized that unless you set objectives very high, you don't achieve anything at all.

Coca-Cola is the most powerful brand on earth. Its red and white logo is readily recognized in almost all areas of the globe. It is tough to figure, then, that at the time of the Lake Placid games, many industry analysts considered Coke to be a stodgy and old brand that had lost considerable luster—and was unsure of its future.

Actually, following the Olympics, the first product endorsement deal I signed was with Coca-Cola. I did a TV commercial for Coke that featured footage from my NHL debut in net for the Atlanta Flames. That night, a home game, we won and I played well. It was just about the best backdrop I could have imagined, with me making saves, my dad cheering for me in the stands, and my teammates slapping me on the back in the locker room afterward.

The commercial had all the right music and it was all warm and fuzzy and feel-good. It won awards. The endorsement commenced a business relationship with Coke that continues for me to this day.

Not long after the commercial hit the airwaves, Coca-Cola began a rapid ascendance to its former place of dominance. But let me tell you something—all of this had nothing to do with the commercial or me. It did, though, have a whole lot to do with a man named Roberto C. Goizueta, a man who knew the importance of having a clearly defined mission, values, and messages.

On March 1, 1981, almost a year to the day that the commercial was filmed, Coca-Cola promoted Goizueta, a Cuban immigrant and longtime Coke employee, from president to chairman of the board and CEO. Over the next 17 years, until his death from cancer, Goizueta led and directed the rapid global growth of Coke, and he created more wealth for its shareholders than any other company in history.

Goizueta succeeded for many reasons. A primary reason was that even before he took over the top job, he had in a drawer in his desk two documents, each two pages: One described what he considered to be the responsibilities of the CEO of Coca-Cola; the other outlined his vision for the future of the company and what was necessary to make that future happen.

Those documents were anchors and the foundation of a worldwide commercial success story. Goizueta kept those documents in his office during his entire tenure as chairman and CEO at Coke. He would occasionally retrieve and edit and recondition the contents of the documents—but fundamental principles and values were fairly constant. In one way or another, through layers of management and corporate decision-making, they cultivated and supported a shared dream and common purpose among the employees of Coca-Cola.

Great Teams Have a Shared Dream: Chapter Recap

- **Make the Quest Epic:** Challenge your people to greatness.
- **Have a Clearly Defined Mission, Values, and Messages:** Because if you don't know where you are going, any path will get you there.
- **Get with the Program—Or Get Out:** Everyone needs to be on board.
- **Leverage Individuality for Team Strength:** Everyone is different—try to make it work for you.
- **Bring People Together—In One Place:** There is only so much team building that can be done over the phone or online. Create the locker room.

3

Great Teams Make Personal Sacrifices

> *No fine work can be done without concentration and self-sacrifice and toil and doubt.*
>
> —MAX BEERBOHM

In the bedlam and joyous hysteria on the ice following our gold medal-clinching win over Finland on February 24, 1980, I searched the stands for my father. As I canvassed the crowd, TV cameras trained in on me as I located first a friend to whom I called out—and the words were easily readable on my lips—"Where's my father?" ABC TV commentator Ken Dryden (one of the greatest goalies ever) helped narrate and gave drama to the scene by telling a national television audience, "There's Jim Craig, looking for his father."

Seconds after I asked the question, Mark Johnson's fiancée, Leslie, who knew where my dad was sitting, took my arm, pointed, and helped me locate him.

My looking for my father got a lot of attention. It shows my love for my father and my urgent desire to share something very special with him. That is a lesson that is all positive.

Jim and his father, Don, shortly after the 1980 Winter Olympics.
Credit: Jim Craig

But I want to dig down a bit more into what was going on in those precious moments—and I want to give background and explanation. In searching and trying to find my father, I was trying to connect with him, yes—but I was also trying to connect with my mother, whom cancer had taken from my family a year and a half prior to the Olympics. It was a spiritual and emotional connection I was trying to make with my mother and father, to thank them for all the sacrifices they made for me. My sacrifices were enabled by their sacrifices. I knew that my father was thinking of my mother—and when my eyes met his eyes a circle of love and years of sacrifice and commitment was joined.

Their sacrifices were about time, hard work, and delivering tough love when necessary—and, when appropriate, doling out tender love, support, and inspiration when I was down and needed a pick-me-up.

No team and no individual can achieve greatness without the personal sacrifice of many.

No team—no one—gets there alone.

■ ■ ■

When I preach and teach the notion of personal sacrifice, I am not talking merely about putting in long hours on the practice field and in the office. It is not just about a willingness to hurt more out on the ice or to get into the classroom early or to study late at the library. I am talking about a far bigger concept. I am talking about a constellation of giving, deprivation, and even suffering. And this sacrifice isn't just about you; it never can be. It is also about all the people around you—your family, your friends, and your mentors. They are all drawn in and sacrifice is demanded from all of them on your path to greatness.

To a man, every player on the 1980 U.S. Olympic hockey team will tell you that their own individual path to Lake Placid and the podium was one supported along the way by many people—and many people had to give their time, love, and commitment to make a dream happen.

And it starts early. I remember my youth hockey days. I launched my career when I was eight years old and in third grade. Easton had a vibrant youth hockey league, with three levels, maybe 20 teams, and hundreds of kids playing. Of course, the league didn't run on its own; it wasn't on autopilot. It was supported by scores of parents and other adults who contributed hundreds of hours every season to organize practices and games—and to shuttle my friends and I to and from rinks. And with so many local towns and cities having their own youth hockey programs—and since there were not many rinks in the area—ice time was at a premium and you took it when you could get it. That meant practice happened before school, at five or six in the morning. So you got up at 4:30 or 5:00 and your parents took shifts driving the kids to one of the rinks, which could be 10 or 15 miles away. They stuck around for practice—and then they drove us home. And then we went to school and they went to work.

Did the uniforms and equipment magically appear? Nope. Someone had to spring for all that—and the funds were drummed up through parents digging deep, us players canning at local supermarkets, local merchants cutting a check, and adults and kids working together to plan and run fundraisers.

Again, it is a constellation of sacrifice.

When you notch it up and dare to try and work for greatness—and this applies no matter in what field you are going for the gold—then the magnitude of sacrifice demands and requires one to hurt physically and emotionally. It will also make emotional demands on those who love and care about you.

Remember that.

■ ■ ■

In this book I want to give a special call out to Steve Janaszak, someone who exemplifies a special and humble form of sacrifice. Steve is the only member of the 1980 U.S. Olympic hockey team that did not play at Lake Placid. I know that we would not have won the gold medal at Lake Placid if Steve Janaszak had not been on our team.

It is also curious that even though Steve did not play at Lake Placid, in the final couple months prior to the games, when several players who would be on the final roster still were in danger of being cut, his position was secure. Herb and Craig Patrick had decided they wanted me to be their number one goaltender in the Olympics. They were also resolute that Steve would be the number two goalie or backup to me. You needed two goaltenders.

Why do I say that we would not have won without Steve? Because without Steve I would not have been able to play at the level I did for those two weeks in February in 1980.

Steve was an exceptional teammate—and that is the reason one of the first comments I made publicly following our gold medal win was to give thanks and praise to Steve for the selfless and supportive role he played for the six months we were together. In good part, I played at my best because Steve played at his best throughout all the practices and pre-Olympic games. He forced me to give 100 percent or lose my starting slot.

You might wonder if this is personal sacrifice or just being a standup person and competitive athlete. I submit that is being standup and a competitor—as well as much more. It is sacrifice. It is a sacrifice to hold in your emotions and try not to pit teammates against teammates, so that, maybe, you gain a political edge that could put you in goal. It was a sacrifice for Steve not to play up his own abilities and accomplishments—which were considerable—and sow a bit a bit of questioning and discord that could have teammates, coaches, and U.S. Hockey administrators wondering if he was the guy that should be between the pipes. Steve engaged in none of that. He sought to make it in net through hard work and preventing goals.

Even more—in all the years since Lake Placid, Steve never sought to develop and push a narrative that he should have seen playing time in the Olympics. He never badmouthed any decisions or said he got a bad deal. Steve unfailingly praised and congratulated the entire team.

Steve Janaszak represents, through and through, the character, spirit, and work ethic that enabled all of us to beat the unbeatable and win the unwinnable.

Understand That Not Only You Sacrifice

As I have said—over and over—none of us gets there alone. And achieving greatness is going to require sacrifice not just from you, but from those who love and support you.

Gold Medal Strategies, the company I founded and for which I serve as president, advises and inspires people and organizations to achieve their full potential. One is bound, entwined, and dependent on the other: people make up organizations; organizations are made up of people. It was about six years ago—in response to a need and a request from individuals and groups—that I began to expand my professional focus from only motivational speaking to also teamwork coaching and sales seminars. With these added dimensions of my business, I am required to have far more personal interaction and do far more one-on-one coaching and mentoring than I did in the past. I enjoy this role and, through it, I am able to deliver enhanced value and competitive advantage. And my own life lessons come into play in my work. These are lessons that spouses and parents the world over can relate to.

It was early in my post-hockey career; Charlie and I had just been married, we both had jobs, and we were busy, but life was not that complicated. My job involved some travel—but we still saw plenty of each other. We saved money and bought a home—and then we bought and built a bigger home. Then JD was born—and three years later came our daughter, Taylor. Charlie worked hard as an all-star stay-at-home mom. With the new responsibilities, I started to work even more hours and focused on making more money. However, while I fiercely loved my wife and children, I lost sight that my most important job was being a husband and father. I thought it was enough that I sacrificed to make money to pay the mortgage on a nice home, to purchase food and clothes, and to be able to drive a nice car. It wasn't.

I neglected to understand the sacrifice that my family was making because of my work and the hours I committed to it. Eventually I woke up and recognized what I was doing. Then I committed myself to an effort to make changes in order to balance my life and work. I remained a success professionally. And I brought my "A" game as a husband and father.

Remain aware that your sacrifice—no matter what arena you are competing in—is not just about you. It will affect those around you. I was able to strike a healthy balance between work and family—but people need to be honest with themselves and with those who love and care about them. The fact is that sometimes the quest and the goal is so lofty that your sacrifice will require from those around you a level of sacrifice that they aren't willing to make. If you don't square things away early on, then you are inviting a lot of problems later.

Talk things over with your support team—whether that team is inside or outside the office. Thorough, open, and honest communication is essential prior to taking the first step on your journey for greatness. You need to be sure if you want to start down that road. And if so—you need to be sure who you will need with you—and whether they are willing to join you for every step of the journey.

Jim and Charlie in front of the Allstate Hall of Fame Mural at USA House at the 2010 Vancouver Winter Olympic Games. The mural, which was created during the games by mural artist Tracy Lee Stum, pays tribute to 15 Olympians, including Jim; two paralympians; and two teams that are in the U.S. Olympic Hall of Fame.

Credit: Jim Craig

■ ■ ■

Director Gavin O'Connor and writer Eric Guggenheim did so much right in creating the movie *Miracle*. Along with the superb performances of Kurt Russell as Herb Brooks and Patricia Clarkson as Patti Brooks, among the emotions and lessons that the film teaches about the journey of our team is that sacrifice needs to be shared if greatness is to be achieved.

There is a scene early in the movie when Herb, his mind knotted with thoughts of hockey, enters the house and casually asks Patti, "Where are the kids?" She responds, "I sold them." The jest doesn't register with Herb and he looks in the refrigerator and says, "We're out of milk."

Soon after, in another scene, the couple has a tiff, one directly tied to Herb's obsession with the past—with being the final player cut on that 1960 team—and his ongoing struggle to come to grips with it and his single-minded focus to coach the right team in the right place at the right moment in history, all of which are making things difficult on his family

"I know what this is about," an exasperated and perturbed Patti Brooks says to Herb. "I know it and you know it."

"What? Know what?" Herb barks back.

"This—what you're doing," responds Patti. "Chasing after something you didn't get—that you may never get. What if it doesn't work out, Herb, huh? Are we gonna do this every four years."

Herb doesn't say anything.

Patti says, "It's okay. Go finish your work. Go."

Herb goes back to his projector, watching hockey films. Soon he returns to talk with Patti. He explains that he needs to do this—to coach this team—and he only knows how to do it one way; he also says he knows it won't be easy on her or the kids.

"Patti, I have to do this," says Herb. "I know you do," his wife responds.

I don't know if this type of exchange actually happened between Herb and Patti in real life. I do know that Herb could be a bear of a man—obstinate, difficult, demanding, and a workaholic—all in pursuit of perfection. He sacrificed a lot. So did his family. But I also know that Herb and Patti had a wonderful marriage and that he relied on her heavily for comfort and support. Herb loved his children, Danny and Kelly, and they adored him. Herb Brooks and his family are an example of successful and shared sacrifice.

■ ■ ■

I admire the grit and determination of Mark Wells. I also admire that he recognized and cared that you don't sacrifice alone.

In 1989, Mark was working in the restaurant industry and he sustained a serious back injury that would leave him in almost constant pain for 12 years, until an innovative laser surgery did its own miracle work and alleviated his agony. Mark is a team player and he got as much out of his natural ability as any of us—so it wasn't surprising when I read how when he lay in bed, following an 11-hour surgery about a month after he suffered the injury, and, though he had next to no mobility and the pain coursed through him, he thought about how his condition would affect his family. He understood that the road ahead would not just be his struggle, but theirs as well.

None of us get there alone.

Sacrifice for Something You Love

There is an old adage: "Find something you love to do and you will never have to work a day in your life."

There is a lot of wisdom and a bit of truth in that statement. It jibes with what soccer star Brandi Chastain said that, "To be honest with you, I never looked at soccer as a sacrifice."

I take stock of that august adage and what Chastain said—but I have a different take on the loving and sacrifice and work angle. I think it is more realistic to say that if you find something you love, then the hard work and sacrifice will be more bearable, and you will be more willing and committed to staying at it. No matter how much you love something, if you want to be great at it then you are going to have to sacrifice, sweat, and hurt. But if you love what you are doing, then you know the sacrifice and hurt is worth it.

I love my wife and children with all my heart. But being a great husband and father takes a lot of effort and it is a job I need to stay after and get better at every day.

Recall that when I was still in junior high, I used to make those Sunday morning trips into Boston to play several hours against top competition. It was hard work and uncomfortable, but I was eager and willing to improve.

I had dreams back then to play big time hockey—yes, college hockey, Olympic hockey, and pro hockey. But even then, when for a young kid all is possible, I knew that there were no guarantees. I stayed after it anyway.

What I emphasize and teach here is that if you are going to make big personal sacrifices, then you better find something that you love and in which you believe. Whether I had any ability or not, I had found something about which I could be truly passionate—and that ensured my willingness to continue sacrificing.

One of the most intense competitors I have met is Doug Flutie, the Heisman Trophy winner and pro football standout.

Let me tell you something about Doug: To him, Heaven is one never-ending game of pickup basketball, football, and baseball. The guy just loves to play sports. He loves to compete. Throughout his entire career he was known as someone who worked extraordinarily hard and gave optimum effort to help his team win. Doug has surely made a very nice living through athletics—but I also know that he couldn't help himself: He had to do what he did. And while those long hours in the weight room, running, and on the football field no doubt were exhausting and exacted a tremendous emotional toll—after all, playing in front of a live audience of 80,000 and millions more watching on television is not relaxing—he was sustained by his love for sport and the energy and thrill he received from it.

What doesn't get played up enough about the 1980 U.S. Olympic hockey team is how much of a bunch of rink rats we all were. We weren't like the Soviets: each selected at a young age by the state and then groomed and developed in a rigid laboratory. Not us—to a player we all started on frozen ponds in our neighborhood or backyard rinks. We found something we loved at an early age—and from there on in you could not keep us away from the game. Prior to high school hockey, when I still played in the youth leagues, not only would my buddies and I practice before school but, during the winter, we would also head to the ponds after school and put in a couple more hours until it got so dark you couldn't see the puck.

■ ■ ■

There is a scene in *Miracle* when about 40 of the remaining players who have tried out for the 1980 U.S. hockey squad are sitting in the bleachers of the rink at the U.S. Olympic Training Center at Colorado Springs. Herb reads off the names of the players who are on the 26-man roster, from which the 20-man roster that will go to Lake Placid will be carved. Those who have just been cut get up and filter out. Herb says to those of us remaining to not feel sorry for them because they were the "lucky" ones.

What did Herb mean by this? What he meant was that they would not be subject to the Spartan and exhausting training regimen that we would. They would not have the wrath of Herb Brooks set upon them—we soon called him, less than affectionately, The Ayatollah.

Herb was letting us know that we were in for it. But I don't know if it is appreciated enough that he knew what he was in for, and committed *himself* to a hard road full of hurt and sacrifice.

Herb Brooks sacrificed for something he loved—but the toll on him was huge. If you just look at the time he spent with our team—not to mention the close to 20 years of chasing and yearning prior to that—you see a man who gave for something he loved.

Winning unto itself—especially in international competition—places a tremendous burden and stress on a coach. But remember that the method that Herb practiced to get the most out of us involved him being the enemy of all of us. He said right from the get-go that he was going to be our coach, but not our friend. He knew that is what he needed to do but I don't think he found it particularly pleasant—quite the opposite. Herb later said that the period he spent coaching us was the loneliest time of his life. I believe it.

Managers and team leaders often have to make that sacrifice—and resist the urge to be a buddy and pal of those they are managing and leading. This might be fun and easy to do, but frequently it is not what is necessary to pull greatness out of people. I don't care who you are—even the hardened soul of Herb Brooks—it is our tendency and our desire to be liked. It is contrary to our instincts to strive not to be liked. You always want to be respected—but not necessarily liked.

■ ■ ■

One more comment on sacrificing for what you love. Did you know that Michael Jordan had a "love of the game" clause in his contract that allowed him to play basketball anytime in the off-season? Jordan was as fierce a competitor and hard worker as they come. He also loved what he did.

Sacrifice for something you love.

Sacrifice for Your Legacy

In the chapter "Members of Great Teams Have a Shared Dream," I advise managers and other corporate leaders and coaches to "make the quest epic." When you communicate to a group and inspire them, when you can invest them with a task of doing something extraordinary, then you increase their chances of bearing up under the stress, long hours, and conflict.

And it can't just be about the money. Now I'm a realist and I know that one can endure a load of hurt and struggle if there is a pot of gold waiting to be grabbed at the end of the journey. But I also know that if you put together a team that is motivated by money *and* the understanding that it is doing something important and worthwhile, then it will beat, every time, a team that is doing it *only* for the money.

Sir Ernest Shackleton, the British polar explorer, knew that to demand people to sacrifice greatly, they had to be presented with a great challenge—especially when next to no money was involved. There is still debate whether Shackleton really posted these famous words in a newspaper want ad recruiting men for his 1914 trans-Arctic expedition (the locus of the debate is that the actual ad has not been located): "Men wanted for hazardous journey. Low wages, bitter cold, long hours of complete darkness. Safe return doubtful. Honor and recognition in event of success."

Whether the ad exists, it is a fact that more than 6,000 men and women in England applied to join Ernest Shackleton on an expedition that was widely and fully understood to be one of great danger and extreme discomfort and which indeed paid only "low wages." It was also an expedition that just might make history. Those 6,000 men and women were willing to risk their lives to establish a legacy of honor and achievement for all time.

■ ■ ■

I do a lot of work with pharmaceutical companies; a considerable portion of that work is talking with, inspiring, and coaching sales forces. If you are a hard-working pharma sales rep you can make a very good living. If you are a hard-working and talented pharma rep you can make even a better living. The money is good—no doubt. But when I speak to these reps I impress upon them that it has to be more than the money; it has to be about building a legacy, giving back, and being part of something that improves lives—something that heals and cures, that allows for more time with loved ones.

Selling a pill and earning a salary and commission is merely about making a living. Selling a cure, alleviating suffering, and keeping people healthy is about making a life.

When you sacrifice to make a life—you sacrifice for your legacy.

Recognize and Show Appreciation for Those Who Sacrifice with You

Lieutenant Colonel Hal Moore is an American hero. In the autumn of 1965, while stationed at Fort Benning in Georgia, he spoke to the men of the U.S. Army First Battalion, Seventh Cavalry—the unit he commanded—prior to it heading to combat in Vietnam. Here is an excerpt from his speech:

> I can't promise that I will bring you all home alive. But this I swear before you and before Almighty God: That when we go into battle, I will be the first to set foot on the field, and I will be the last to step off. And I will leave no one behind. Dead or alive, we will all come home together. So help me God.

There is no more sincere and honorable example of recognizing and showing appreciation for the personal sacrifice of your unit, team, or employees than to share that sacrifice—and to be among them.

Of course, thankfully, recognizing and showing appreciation for other's sacrifice does not require the heroism and selflessness of Hal Moore. But we can learn from his example. If you are a manager and you want your employees to work long and hard over the weekend or late into the evening—then you best be willing to share the workload with them over those hours. There is no better gift you can give to your employees or your co-workers than to share in their efforts and to show appreciation for their efforts.

Work with and alongside them. Labor is sacred.

Another way you recognize and show appreciation for sacrifice is through rewards and publicizing the efforts of players and employees. Set the goal and then establish a policy and program of incentives and rewards for achieving standards en route to the goal—and then for reaching the goal itself.

In many ways I'm in the *showing appreciation* business. Most of the events and seminars for which I'm hired are some form of giving thanks to employees and vendors and company reps. I experience first-hand the benefits and boosts in productivity and organizational improvement that result from people feeling appreciated, their toil and labor being touted and talked about. Your team will not do anything great if it feels it is going to sacrifice day after day and not be recognized and rewarded.

■ ■ ■

Vince Lombardi ranks as one of the best team builders in history; he built the dynasty of the Green Bay Packers. Today, organizations from across many sectors study the team-building methodology of Lombardi. Lombardi understood the value of thinking of an athletic team as a family—and he understood that the extended family included the wives and children of the players. Lombardi knew that all family members shared the sacrifice necessary to produce greatness. It was with this understanding that every season he purchased special gifts for all the wives—including mink stoles, TVs, jewelry, and even sterling silver tea sets.

When you look at the record of Vince Lombardi and the Green Bay Packers, those tokens of appreciation appear to have done some good.

Beyond the Ice—Other Mentors and Coaches

All sacrifice is relative. And I want to make certain that I recognize there are special people whose sense of sacrifice, and the sacrifices to which they commit, are infinitely more valuable and admirable than those of athletes, business people, and politicians. Of course, the people I'm talking about are our men and women in the armed forces.

I am fortunate to have worked with many highly successful business people who have also worn the uniform—men like Michael Minogue, the CEO of Abiomed and a former Army Ranger and graduate of West Point; U.S. Navy SEAL commander Thomas Chaby; Dennis Falci, Director of U.S. Managed Markets Sales and Training for Aventis and a U.S. Army veteran—and many others. I admire these men greatly and I believe that the sacrifices they have made for this country and for their fellow service people provide high-level value and competitive advantage for the companies with which they are employed.

Every single person who goes into the military stares down the barrel of a gun; I don't care if you ever hear a single shot fired in anger. Every service person sacrifices something; some sacrifice all.

And their sacrifice illustrates clearly that notion I talk about— about the personal sacrifice being a shared sacrifice. When a mother or father, a sister or brother, a son or daughter, goes off to serve, there is a sacrifice made by all those who love them and remain at home.

We see in the men and women of our armed forces, and the families who love them, the most sublime and purest and sacred form of personal sacrifice. There is much that all of us can learn from their example.

■ ■ ■

There are other examples that are helpful to study and that are inspiring and useful when urging and calling for personal sacrifice.

In May 2007, I delivered a keynote address at the Minneapolis Convention Center for Fairview Health Services, one of the leading not-for-profit health service providers in the Midwest. The event I spoke at was Fairview's annual meeting of employees and vendors. Fairview did a great job of putting together a roster of speakers and presenters, all of whom delivered a different message and a different value.

Hiring me made sense for a number of reasons—one of which I will admit is that Minnesota is about as hockey crazy a land as you can get. It is Hockey U.S.A. And let's remember that 13 of the 20 players on the 1980 U.S. Olympic hockey team were from Minnesota. Fairview Health Services charged me with the task of inspiring its group for the year ahead—all the while enlisting some of that psychic energy from one of the greatest episodes in U.S. sports history—which wouldn't have happened, of course, without the contributions of the native sons of the North Star State.

Speaking after me was a gentleman named Nando Parrado. I provided one type of speech and Parrado would deliver another type. He would put in context the notion of personal sacrifice.

Nando Parrado was one of 45 passengers on a chartered plane that crashed in a remote section of the Andes Mountains in Argentina on Friday, October 13, 1972.

On impact 12 people died; five more died within a day of the crash. Everyone on the plane sustained some sort of injury. With little food left, and facing high altitude and high winds and temperatures that dipped to 20 degrees below zero Fahrenheit—all conditions which taxed mind and body and rapidly ate up calories—the hopes of anyone surviving was about nil. Nine days into the ordeal (a day after another passenger died), and facing certain starvation, the survivors made a decision to eat the flesh of the dead. A few days later, the survivors heard crackling from a radio transmitter salvaged from the plane that a search and rescue mission for them had been called off because of the danger involved and because there was just about no chance anyone could have survived the crash.

On the 60th day after the crash, Parrado and Roberto Canessa set out to locate help. They marched and trekked for 10 days over and through mountainous and treacherous terrain before meeting up with a Chilean farmer. The farmer called the police and Parrado and Canessa guided a search party to the 14 survivors still at the crash site. Twenty-nine people died in the disaster—including Nando Parrado's mother and sister.

New England Patriots coach Bill Belichick, one of the biggest winners in society, is a good friend of mine. I met Bill a few years ago at a charity event in which we both participated. We stayed in touch, and we correspond frequently. Bill and I are fellow boating, deep-sea fishing, and ocean enthusiasts. He has a home on Nantucket, which is a short boat ride from where my family lives on the south coast of Massachusetts. During the summer, Charlie and I will take our boat over to Nantucket and meet up with Bill.

Bill appreciates the value of enlisting stories of epic human endurance and survival to build a team and to put the concept of personal sacrifice in perspective. Bill was inspired with the man, Ernest Shackleton, and his trans-Arctic journey, both which I mentioned earlier in this chapter.

In the summer of 2001, Bill and his family took in the documentary film, *Shackleton's Antarctic Adventure*, at the IMAX, a giant screen and high resolution theater at the Museum of Science in Boston. Bill was blown away by the documentary. It's no wonder.

The documentary tells the truly miraculous and unbelievable true story of Shackleton and his 27-man crew that set sail from England in December 1914, with the goal of making the first crossing of the Antarctic continent. It was the start of an odyssey in which the men and their ship would be bumped around in Antarctic ice for 10 months before the ice finally crushed the ship; they would then camp exposed for five months on an ice floe; they then sailed in three small boats to set up camp on Elephant Island, the first bit of land they had been on in 492 days. But Elephant Island was not in any shipping lanes. Shackleton knew that to stay there meant death—so he and five other men embarked on an 800-mile journey on a life raft, through some of the world's most violent seas, to reach a whaling station at a place called South Georgia Island. They made it—but on the other side of the island from where the station was located. So Shackleton and two others, all frostbitten and on the verge of starvation, marched 26 miles over mountains and glaciers to reach the station. Once there they boarded boats and picked up the two men on the shore of South Georgia Island. They then sailed to rescue the men at Elephant Island. Twenty-one months after The Endurance left England, Shackleton rescued his 22 men at Elephant Island.

All 28 men who left England survived.

Bill was so impressed with the film and the story it told that he arranged for a special IMAX screening of *Shackleton's Antarctic Adventure* for the entire New England Patriots team during the hot and muggy days of August training camp.

"This was a story and adventure that was about the epitome of teamwork and sacrifice and working for one another," Bill told me. "The camaraderie and giving and unity of effort of Shackleton and his men was what my staff and I were trying to achieve with the Patriots. I wanted the team to see the movie—together."

So what was the reaction of a group of multimillionaire athletes to the documentary?

"It resonated with all of them—and the message hit home," said Bill.

We know how the following season ended, with the Patriots in the Super Bowl in New Orleans and facing their own daunting task—albeit beyond minuscule and minor in comparison to what the Shackleton voyage faced—in taking on the heavily-favored and high-scoring St. Louis Rams. I saw so much of the 1980 U.S. Olympic hockey team in the Patriots in that game. (Remember, Bill Belichick has, perched on a chair in his office and facing his desk, a framed photo of the on-ice celebration of our team after we beat the Soviets.) The Pats did not have the individual talent of the Rams—but Bill and his staff had designed just the right game plan to optimize the strengths of the Patriots and hamper and throw off the Rams. New England executed superbly on the field—and New England won its first Super Bowl.

Early in the 2002–2003 season, *ESPN* did a special segment on the motivational skills of Bill Belichick. Andrea Kremer, host of the segment, said, "Last year, the team's trip to see the story of Shackleton's Antarctic expedition got a lot of play—but Belichick told me he still heard players referring to it when the weather got bad late in the season. They were saying, 'We can't be wusses when those guys were in the cold for almost two years.'"

That Bill Belichick is one heck of a coach.

Great Teams Make Personal Sacrifices—Chapter Recap

- **Understand That Not Only You Sacrifice:** You are not in it alone. Your sacrifice will have an impact on those around you. Make sure the shared sacrifice is understood and appreciated before starting on your journey.
- **Sacrifice for Something You Love:** It can't just be about money or hopes of fame. You will best be able to bear the sacrifice when it is in pursuit of something you love and which you feel is important.
- **Sacrifice for Your Legacy:** Sacrifice for something epic— and for something noble and good that you will transmit to this world and which will endure.
- **Recognize and Show Appreciation for Those Who Sacrifice with You:** Rewards and incentives—and at least the hope of recognition—inspire and support sacrifice.

4

Great Teams Hold Themselves and Others Accountable

Some favorite expressions of small children: "It's not my fault. They made me do it. . . . I forgot." Some favorite expressions of adults: "It's not my job. No one told me. It couldn't be helped." True freedom begins and ends with personal accountability.

—DAN ZADRA

Do you recognize the name Gary Smith? Probably not. But if you are any sort of sports fan, you have seen the image of Gary Smith over and over.

Gary Smith was an important member of the 1980 U.S. Olympic hockey team. "Smitty" wasn't a player; he wasn't a coach. He was the athletic trainer for the team. And like every member of the team, he did his job. If he didn't do his job, we may not have won at Lake Placid. That's the truth.

So when did you see Smitty? Think of Mike Eruzione scoring the go-ahead, and eventual winning, goal against the Soviet Union. Think of the next few moments of footage, of the bedlam and celebrating. You remember that guy on the U.S. bench, the guy pumping his fists, a white towel in his hand; he had the eyeglasses with the big lenses and dark rims; he had on that blue pullover with USA stitched on it. That is Smitty.

Gary Smith was the trainer of the University of Minnesota hockey team when Herb Brooks was its coach. The two men worked well together. When Herb was named coach of the 1980 U.S. team, the USOC let him know that it had assigned him a trainer. Herb said thanks but let the USOC know that the team already had a trainer. Like everyone else on the team, Herb picked Smitty for a reason.

As I said, Smitty did his job. He actually did multiple jobs.

Smitty was accountable—and he held others accountable. His smart thinking, and accountability, may have saved the Soviet game.

During that game, we were a few seconds away from killing a penalty. With those few seconds remaining, Neil Broten jumped the gun, so to speak, and was on his way over the boards, and a referee was watching him. If Neil had made it on to the ice, we almost certainly would have been called for too many men on the ice—and the Soviet power play would have been extended for two more minutes. Not good: the most potent and highest scoring power play on earth, given more time. But Neil didn't make it on to the ice, and that's because Smitty saw what was happening and he pulled him back on to the bench. Herb was watching, and he walked down to Smitty and said, "Way to stay in the game, Smitty."

Every member of the team is a component of success.

Every member of the team needs to be accountable—and to hold others accountable.

Then again, in Smitty's case, being accountable and doing his job didn't always solicit a figurative pat on the back from Herb.

There was that episode following the pre-Olympic game in Norway against the Norwegian national team, a team that did not nearly have the talent that we had. We had played without enthusiasm and drive, and we tied the Norwegians, 2-2. Herb was furious. He assembled the team on the ice after the game, and had it do sprints up and back on the ice, over and over and over. Doing a few minutes of this is exhausting, but he kept it going for 20 minutes. At this point, the manager of the rink, who did not speak English, gestured to Smitty, who did not speak Norwegian, that he needed to lock up. Smitty had the unhappy task of having to tell this to Herb. Herb, still vibrating with anger, fixed his stare of daggers on Smitty and said, "Get me the f-ing keys and I'll lock up." Smitty went back to the rink manager and, through gestures, asked for the manager's keys, but the manager wouldn't give them up. He did, though, turn off the lights in the rink and left.

Smitty rejoined the rest of us—in the dark.

There were those final minutes in the Soviet game, and the emotion and energy were already over the top and continuing to build and grow. We were on the precipice of history. One of the biggest upsets in the annals of athletics was within our grasp. How were we to hold on and get it done and bring it home? The answer was to hold ourselves accountable.

"Play your game . . . play your game," Herb Brooks kept reminding us as the seconds ticked away.

■ ■ ■

Holding yourself accountable is about doing your job, not looking for an out, and getting things done no matter how hard you have to work or sacrifice. How about holding others accountable? What does that mean? Is that a nice way for describing a career advancing strategy of deflecting blame or responsibility, or dumping it on someone else? Not at all.

Everyone in an organization needs to have a vested interest in the total output and total product. You can be the hardest working, best-prepared, and smartest employee in the world, but if you can't speak up and let others know that you observe things are going well, then the organization is not operating effectively. As well, you need to be open to others holding you accountable.

And to hold others accountable, you had better be prepared to help them be accountable.

Accountable, Yes. But for What?

First you need to have a game plan in place and figure out who is accountable for what. Back in 1980, each and every player's role was clearly defined. We all knew what was expected of us. We knew where we were supposed to be at what point in a play; we understood the options available to us; we recognized what was expected and were accountable.

You need to understand what is expected of you—and then prepare to meet expectations. If you skate on to ice or walk in to the office wondering what you are accountable for, then your team has problems.

■ ■ ■

Early in 2010, Milprint, a division of The Bemis Company, the biggest flexible food-packaging manufacturer in the Americas, was still trying to get its arms around accountability issues. A major reason for this uncertainty and instability was that it really was not just one team but rather two teams.

In March of 2010, Bemis acquired Alcan, a competitor. For Milprint, this basically doubled its size overnight. Forty-five days after they closed on the acquisition, Milprint scheduled a "One Team—One Mission" event in Naples, Florida. The meeting was a component of the process of melding Milprint and Alcan together and to get what were once two organizations operating as one under the Milprint name.

Indeed, the process was not yet on firm footing. Roles were not yet established, and important responsibilities had not yet been assigned or assumed.

Bemis hired me to speak at the "One Team—One Mission" event.

Bryan Brandt, VP of Sales for Milprint, told me, "We want you to help inspire everyone to let down their guard and to stop being so territorial. We need open and honest communication among all our employees if we are to eliminate the old ways of doing things and take the best of each company and create a great new team. I also want your speech to throw strong support behind Don Nimis (the President of Milprint) as he takes charge and leads this process."

Bryan also said he wanted me to challenge the group, to inspire and charge them with the task of coming together and sharing a goal of becoming one team. I was scheduled to speak early in the afternoon, and that night I would have dinner with Bryan and Don Nimis; this dinner was another important element in getting Milprint on track. During the dinner, Bryan wanted me to challenge Don to take the lead, provide a vision and build a team. These up-close and in-person opportunities with management enable me to emphasize poignantly and intensely what needs to be done to get members of a team sharing an objective—and oftentimes what I coach and emphasize is the *urgency* of what needs to be done. In my preparation and research for my appearance for Milprint, it was obvious to me that a sense of urgency was needed.

Jim in his element, the teacher and coach, addressing a corporate meeting.
Credit: Jim Craig

If I accomplished nothing else in Naples but to jump-start everyone—and to make sure everyone knew that every second they weren't coming together was a second wasted and a second lost to the competition—then I delivered, and then some.

My speech to Milprint was a bit more "rah-rah" than normal and full of language that challenged—and maybe even confronted. But I could tell I was getting through. If people were uneasy, well, that was all right—as long as their minds remained open. To be uneasy and to shut your mind down, that is a prescription for failure.

At dinner with Don and Bryan, I stayed after the importance of starting now to make sure that everyone knew what was expected of them—and that expectations needed to be met.

A few days after the event in Naples, I received a note from Bryan Brandt—here are excerpts:

> ... You set the stage for the balance of the meeting. I basically scripted out the rest of the meeting minute by minute. It all focused around on what you did Sunday, continuing to build a team, educating people on the new company, and then learn about the direction of our company (our vision/mission)—this was the unknown going into the meeting.
>
> I had a number of people throughout the meeting saying, "I can't wait to get back and get going ... We are going to kick the crap out of our enemy."
>
> You definitely rattled Don's cage on Sunday. He said he has never been so impacted by a presentation like that before. But then you got in his face at dinner (you gave him an out, which was nice of you), but you shook his world that night. After dinner, he went back to his room early and worked on a vision for *his* company. The next day (Monday) he presented with more energy than I have ever seen. Monday night, he pulled me aside and said how amazed he was with what was being accomplished right in front of his eyes. He told me how impressed he was that I knew this is what we needed, for sticking my neck out, and putting every little detail together.

He apologized for not seeing it and thanked me for pushing for this.

What was confirmed in Bryan's note was that some cage rattling and table pounding (*light* table pounding) was in order. Milprint is going to do great things—and it is going to be a great team. There is much to be impressed about with the people at Milprint, among them that so many were open to coaching and to being challenged.

What Milprint also has going for it is smart and well-intentioned leadership. Don Nimis giving Bryan Brandt so much responsibility and so much deference in the all-important chore of getting the ship righted and on course speaks volumes for the qualities of both men. Of course, it helps that Bryan was right about so much in his strategizing and planning. As well, it is tremendously admirable that Don Nimis, the President, has the humility and character to admit when he may not have recognized what needed to be done—and then when what needed to be done was presented to him, he gave credit where credit was due, and immediately took over and led.

When I returned home, I signed a replica of the jersey I wore in the Soviet game, and I sent it to Don Nimis along with a handwritten note in which I delivered a bit more inspiration and guidance, and also a call to action.

Bet on Bemis, Milprint.

Pull Potential Out of People

When people are trying to skirt an issue or are considering themselves slick and able to fool others, even if what they are doing and their motives are easily understandable, I like to remind them that, "Even if your head is in the sand, that doesn't mean that your butt isn't showing.'

I like to help get people's head out of the sand and make them confront what needs to be confronted. I like them to face what needs to be faced in order that they may fulfill and reach their potential.

A lot has been made about the psychology test that Herb Brooks administered to our team—and that I was the only one on the team that didn't take the test.

In the media, and more broadly in our culture, the tale is told that I protested taking the test and the reason I did so was because I felt the questions and whatever answers I provided were not important or relevant to how I would perform in the net. That is only part of the story. I was doubtful that answering those questions was going to help coaches evaluate my ability and worth to the team, but I had a bigger and more overriding reason for not taking the test: I wanted Herb to cut me so that I could sign an NHL contract and make some money and help my family and myself out.

You see, maybe a week or so prior to Herb assigning the test, my dad had lost his job. He was still mourning the loss of my mother, and he had my two younger brothers still at home. I was worried about my family, and I was not confident at all that playing in the Olympics was going to be a winning experience or one that would result in a medal of any type. So, if I got booted I could ink a contract with the team that had drafted me, the Atlanta Flames. Even if I got sent to the minors I would still have a steady paycheck and my room and board paid for, and I could send money home.

As well, in that I had played internationally for the U.S., even if not in the Olympics, I would have fulfilled a pledge I made to my mother that if I ever had an opportunity to represent my country I would seize and take advantage of that opportunity.

Not taking the test was my chance to get out of Dodge.

But I wasn't going anywhere because Herb knew what I was up to. He wasn't going to cut me. I was going to Lake Placid.

Potential was pulled out of me. I was held accountable.

■ ■ ■

Not long after I had retired from hockey, I was fortunate to land a job at Valassis Inserts, a major producer of the consumer coupon inserts that you find in newspapers. My job was to sell insert space to consumer product companies. It is a highly competitive business—and I enjoyed the job.

In 1986, about a year after I started at Valassis, the company was bought by an Australian media magnate, Kerry Packer, and his company Consolidated Holdings. Among Packer's early decisions was to promote a senior manager named Dave Brandon to CEO. Brandon, a former football player at the University of Michigan, had started at Valassis at a junior level in 1979, quickly become a star, and in only a few years he was a senior executive playing a leading role in the rapid growth of the company.

Dave was a highly personable, warm, results-oriented—and accountable—executive. He introduced himself to and met with every hire, from the junior to senior level. People enjoyed working for Dave; they performed better and the company benefited as a result. It soon became apparent that making Dave the CEO was the right move. Indeed, Kerry Packer, one of the most astute business people on the planet, and very hands-on as an owner, was not like that at all in his relationship with Dave. Packer didn't need to hold Dave Brandon accountable because Dave Brandon held himself accountable.

Valassis had winning ownership and leadership. All was possible.

However, I was up against it. You see, Consolidated Holdings had a hiring policy for sales people and management that all but required a hire to have a college degree. I had left BU one semester short of graduating to chase international hockey glory, and I had not gone back to earn my degree. As well, Dave Brandon thought I was doing a good job, but he thought I could do much, much better.

It seemed my job was in jeopardy.

So this is what happened. Dave Brandon stepped in to become my mentor. He also made me accountable.

Dave told me that I had a job but it would be on a probationary basis. He was going to work closely with me to make me a better salesperson. He would help me—and I needed to work hard and help myself. It would be accountability back and forth.

When this arrangement was first presented to me, I was ticked off. No way. This was like Herb Brooks coming up to me following the blowout at Madison Square Garden and telling me I was being sat down. It was unfair.

But Herb had a plan. So did Dave Brandon.

I became better because of both men.

There were so many lessons I learned from Dave while he mentored me at Valassis. One lesson I learned early on was that telling "Jim Craig and gold medal and Olympic and NHL" stories were no substitute for smart and strategic selling. Yeah, you could do all right with those, but relying on them would not make you a great salesperson. I needed to practice and become an expert at the selling skills that would win business and take care of clients, whether I had ever played any sport or laced up a pair of skates.

Dave believed in consultative selling—that is working with a client or potential client and forging a relationship in which you listened as much as you talked. You asked probing questions. Dave said that the more you listened and the more fruitful the dialogue with a business, the more able you are to offer products and services and solutions from which it can benefit. And when you provide business a benefit, you are doing more than making a sale, you are building trust and a relationship.

I had not been doing much consultative selling. I would walk in to a company and talk about what I had to sell and why the company should buy what I was selling. I would throw in an anecdote or two about the Soviet game or the thrill of making it to the pros, and then I would basically want people to purchase. I had been making a living that way, but I wasn't doing nearly as well for Valassis, or myself, as I could.

Dave became my coach. He also had me take courses in selling and marketing given by outside organizations that Valassis paid for. Dave did his job and I did mine. And, you know, I became better and more effective. Soon I was one of the top producing salespeople in the company. I took over the Northeast U.S. region for Valassis.

I won Salesman of the Year for Valassis. In the 10 years I headed up its Northeast sector, its annual sales grew from $300,000 to $50 million and it became the top producing region for the company.

Dave Brandon left Valassis in 1989 to become the CEO of Domino's. He succeeded in selling pizza just like he did in selling coupons. At the center of this success were teamwork and accountability. Dave made strategic changes that strengthened the company, including starting a recruiting program (you always need to pick the right players), instituting a profit sharing system in which everyone in the company would be rewarded when Domino's did well, and adding classroom instruction to the in-store training that was already in place for employees.

Dave continued his winning ways as a person as well. He always gave a lot of himself to philanthropic events. He and his wife Jan are also generous with their money in supporting worthy causes. In 2006, they gave $4 million to the University of Michigan, with half of that money dedicated to a neonatal intensive care center named for their twin sons Nick and Chris. Doctors at the university saved the boys from a rare and life-threatening blood disease they were born with in 1980.

In the spring of 2010, Dave Brandon was named athletic director at the University of Michigan (he remains on the board of directors at Domino's as chairman). The university's athletic program and the Wolverines are in good hands.

In late winter of 2009, I went back to BU, after almost 30 years away, and I finished up that coursework over the next few months and earned my bachelor's degree. One of the first people I contacted to tell the news was Dave Brandon.

Accountability Is a Two-Way Street

The 1980 U.S. Olympic hockey team did not have high PDI—and this enabled both the coaches to hold the athletes, and the athletes to hold the coaches, accountable.

First off, in the event you are not familiar with PDI, I will explain it. PDI is short for Power Distance Index—a measurement developed by a Dutch organizational sociologist named Geert Hofstede. In cultures with high PDI, such as South Korea (more on this later in the chapter), Morocco, Mexico, and the Philippines, people who hold junior positions in organizations are inhibited and not inclined to question authority. In countries with low PDI, such as the United States, Australia, and Ireland, people are far more inclined and less hesitant to question authority.

Successful organizations need to have low PDI.

The 1980 U.S. Olympic hockey—from top to bottom—had attitude and powerful personalities, and people could speak up and be counted. Sometimes, for sure, we would use Craig Patrick as a filter to communicate with Herb, but we knew we could get the message to him. We would also go to Herb directly. And the reverse was obviously true.

At the beginning of our journey together, members of the 1980 U.S. Olympic hockey team were primarily accountable to themselves, not each other. Almost every one of us had a dream—an "endgame"—to play in the NHL. The endgame was not to win an Olympic gold medal; heck, a medal of any type was a fantasy.

We became accountable to one another and that enabled history to be made.

The environment and working conditions of our team were conducive for accountability. We may have called our coach the "Ayatollah," but in truth, while our organization had a "supreme leader," conversation and suggestions from everyone were encouraged and heeded. There was not a rigid hierarchy. If someone thought he had a better way to do something, then "let's hear it." If someone wasn't doing his job, you would let him know. Of course he would let you know if you weren't doing yours.

I'll refer to and reflect on a couple of well-known exercises of accountability that took place on our team, both of which are dramatized in the Disney movie *Miracle*.

It was only a couple of weeks prior to our first game in the Olympics, and Herb was still bringing in players for consideration. Here we had 20 players who had been together for six months, and Herb was keeping it open that some of us might lose our positions. Now, here, you might say that this is good, not allowing anyone to get comfortable, and using this discomfort to keep us fine-tuned and giving maximum effort. But at that point in our journey together, the disruption and negative energy outweighed positives. Something had to be done. Having a system in place, in which holding each other accountable was expected, made that something possible.

Mike Eruzione and Jack O'Callahan were appointed to let Herb and Craig Patrick know our views. They explained our concerns. They let our coaches know enough was enough, and the team should be set. Twenty guys had worked and sacrificed together, we were in synch, we were committed to one another—and we were a family.

Herb and Craig agreed. Our roster was final for Lake Placid.

Let's now go to that episode in the locker room during the first intermission of the United States—Sweden game, our first game of the Olympics. Rob McClanahan had sustained a deep thigh bruise in the first period and he, in consultation with our team physician, Dr. Nagobads, had decided that he was through for that game. Rob was a great competitor, but he also had a future to think about; he had signed a contract with the Buffalo Sabres. Rob was thinking, "Why put my NHL career in jeopardy?

We needed Rob though—and Herb knew it. The players were already in the locker room. Herb had not joined us yet. In the hallway outside the locker room, Herb talked with Dr. Nagobads. Herb learned that it would be extremely painful for Rob to play with the bruise, but that he would not further injure it.

That made up Herb's mind: Rob was playing.

And Herb was going to hold Rob accountable.

Herb was none too happy with our performance in the first period—and he wasn't happy that Rob was bowing out. Herb got into the locker room and he was seething. He tossed a few choice and well-considered comments this way and that way—and then he zoned in on Rob, who was sitting on a trainer's table in his underwear, his equipment off, and an ice pack on his thigh. (Disney did a good job portraying this event—but since the movie was intended for a family audience, some of the conversation had to be, let's see, *translated* into Rated PG language.)

"What the hell is the matter with *you?*" Herb said to Rob.

"Doc says I'm injured; I can't play," Rob replied.

"Put your gear on!!" Herb said in a steady and firm tone.

"Doc says I can't play."

"LISTEN—I HAVE NO TIME FOR QUITTERS!" Herb yelled. "YOU CAKE EATER! GET ON YOUR GEAR!"

What happened next is instructive. You see, for sure, what was going on, was that Herb was holding Rob accountable. But an element of us holding Herb accountable was about to stir—and quickly explode. This wouldn't have happened if our team had high PDI.

Many of us starting protesting, yelling back at Herb, letting him know that he was out of line. Rob defended himself, bellowing, "I'M NOT A QUITTER!"

If we were not able to hold Herb accountable—or at least try to hold Herb accountable—for the way he addressed us, it would have been too easy for his criticism and abusive language to foment dissent among ourselves, and to weaken our team because we would feel powerless. We did not feel powerless. Jumping back at Herb strengthened the bond of our unit.

"I WANT YOU TO BE A HOCKEY PLAYER!" screamed Herb.

At the same decibel level as Herb was yelling, Rob yelled, "I AM A HOCKEY PLAYER!"

All hell was breaking loose. We were yelling at Herb, and Herb was yelling at Rob. Finally, Rob shouted, "DAMN IT!! YOU WANT ME TO PLAY!! I'LL PLAY!!"

Herb, amid the bedlam, turned for the door. I had a seat near the door. Just prior to opening the door, Herb gave me a wink. Then he said to Craig Patrick, who was standing near me, "That oughta get 'em."

It sure did. Rob put his gear on and returned to the ice for the second period.

So who scored the game-winning goal in the gold medal-clinching game against Finland? Why, that would be Rob McClanahan.

Beyond the Ice—Other Mentors and Coaches

Let's get back to low PDI.

PDI particularly interests me, and I think it is of particular value to discuss, because culture is fundamental to success and failure in almost all areas of life. You can be Einstein brilliant, as innovative as Washington Carver, and have a work ethic like Thomas Edison, but if you don't mesh with a culture then you are bound to fail.

I had never heard of PDI before I started reading Malcolm Gladwell, a brilliant writer, observer, and social commentator. Gladwell has written bestselling books, including *Outliers: The Story of Success*. In *Outliers*, Gladwell takes a more insightful look at why people succeed and don't succeed; he peels back the layers of the onion. The first chapter of *Outliers* focuses on, interestingly enough, a factor that connects almost all of the best Junior League hockey players in Canada.

But it was the seventh chapter of the book, the one titled "The Ethnic Theory of Plane Crashes," in which PDI is discussed, that caught my attention in terms of how it relates to culture and accountability. Some cultures are tough to crack, and there are cultures that don't make it easy to open and keep open a two-way street of accountability.

"The Ethnic Theory of Plane Crashes" is about how culture undermined accountability in the cockpit of passenger planes and led to disaster, over and over.

I don't agree with everything that Malcolm Gladwell presents and argues for in *Outliers*, but I surely agree with some of it. And in

Outliers, he doesn't just show you success to back up his theories, but he shows failure as well—and then shows what was done to turn failure into success.

An example of "failure to success" that he writes about is the history of Seoul-based Korean Airlines (Korean Air) from its launch in 1972 until the late 1990s. During that period, the airline had seven deadly plane crashes, a crash frequency that far exceeded any other airline. It is compelling reading—and is of tremendous value for anyone who cares and wants to know more about how culture can affect a company or any type of organization.

I read more on the crashes, in addition to what was in *Outliers*. One story that I got my hands on, an August 26, 2009, *USA Today* article, called the crashes "a national embarrassment and prompted the Korean government to push for management and operational changes . . ."

Gladwell explains other consequences and reactions:

In April 1999, Delta Air Lines and Air France suspended their flying partnerships with Korean Air. In short order the U.S. Army, which maintains thousands of troops in South Korea, forbade its personnel from flying with the airline. South Korea's safety rating was downgraded by the U.S. Federal Aviation Authority, and Canadian officials informed Korean Air's management that they were considering revoking the company's overflight and landing privileges in Canadian airspace.

What was going on? How come Korean Air had such a scary "loss" rate? It seemed that the planes were in good shape and properly maintained. Pilots were healthy and had the necessary hundreds of hours of flight training. What was the problem?

A main problem was—and Gladwell breaks it all down and lays it out—that there was an aspect of the South Korean culture that interfered with pilots being accountable to one another, and this, of course, meant they were not accountable to the passengers either. It had nothing to do with work ethic or doing the job a pilot felt was his job. And, really, it had very little to do with pilots being responsible. They were being as responsible as they understood they should be.

Again, it had to do with culture. You can never overestimate the importance and consequences of culture on any type of group or organization. Gladwell noted that the most common airline accident "involves seven consecutive human errors," and that the "kinds of errors that cause plane crashes are invariably errors of teamwork and communication." In the case of Korean Airlines, culture increased the chance for error, and it disrupted teamwork and communication—and accountability.

There were a lot of studies and reviews and evaluations of the Korean Air plane crashes. Flight patterns were pored over and weather conditions analyzed. Events in the lives of the pilots prior to the crash were considered. The mechanics of the planes and maintenance records were looked at. And, of course, the cockpit voice recordings—those preserved in the "Black Boxes"—were listened to, studied, and analyzed.

When everything was evaluated, listened to, and pondered, what seemed to be a primary reason that Korean Airlines' planes were crashing so frequently was a culture of subordinates not being able to challenge and hold superiors accountable. Planes were crashing because captains, the senior pilots, were making mistakes, and co-pilots were hesitant to speak up and explain a mistake was being made. A co-pilot was restrained from holding a captain accountable.

On the two-way street of accountability, subordinates and junior staffers need to be able to speak up and not feel they are going to take a hit for doing so. One Korean Air co-pilot, who did speak up to a captain, literally took a hit: the pilot smacked the offending co-pilot in the nose.

As I noted earlier, and Gladwell details this in the chapter, South Korea, Morocco, Mexico, and the Philippines are countries that have a high PDI. Gladwell writes, "Power distance is concerned with attitudes toward hierarchy, specifically with how much a particular culture values and respects authority." In a high PDI country, such as South Korea, employees are far more likely to be afraid to voice their opinion or view to a superior if that opinion or view might correct or contradict the position or decision of the superior.

A postscript here. Korean Airlines took care of its problems. Beginning in 1999, with Cho Yang-Ho (who received his MBA from the University of Southern California) at the helm as chairman, it aggressively instituted changes. As reported in the *USA Today* story, "Korean Air voluntarily chose to comply with some U.S. standards in addition to Korean aviation regulations, including cockpit crew work-and-rest guidelines. It hired Boeing and Airbus for full-flight simulator training. Young pilots are 'now trained to speak up when it's time to speak up,' Cho says."

Korean Air is growing fast—and it is safe. As of the summer of 2010 it has not had a crash in more than 10 years. It continues to invest in safety, and it is upgrading its fleet and buying new planes. It is now the world's largest commercial cargo airline carrier and flies from more cities in the United States to Asia than any other airline.

Great Teams Hold Themselves and Others Accountable— Chapter Recap

- **Accountable, Yes. But for What?:** It is difficult to be accountable when you don't know what is expected of yourself or others within an organization. Get it figured out.
- **Pull Potential Out of People:** Challenge people to recognize and meet their responsibilities—to themselves and others.
- **Accountability Is a Two-Way Street:** If you hold others accountable, be willing to be held accountable. No one is too big or too small to be held accountable.

5

Great Teams Are the Product of Picking the Right Players

A championship team is a team of champions.

—Unknown

If you are a champion manager or coach or administrator, you don't have to be sold on the notion that winning in your category doesn't happen without the right people. It all starts with people. They are your most valuable resource.

From my time playing hockey, and working with organizations and leaders across many different industries and environments, and in studying and analyzing what works in selecting the right players for the team and organization, I have honed in on fundamentals, principles, and philosophies that are the bedrock for building successful teams.

Great teams are the product of picking the right players.

Thorough and gifted recruiters surround themselves with people who make everyone better. They hire people who improve the organization. There is a Silicon Valley tenet that says that "'A' people hire 'A' people, and 'B' people hire 'C' people." The best want the best around them and working for them—and not just the best people but also the *right* people.

Among the most important mentors in my life are those who are also the best recruiters: my parents (they picked one another), all my coaches, including, of course, Herb Brooks, and also the business leaders for whom I've worked. When I was employed by Valassis Communications, my boss was Dave Brandon. He became an important mentor of mine; he showed me how to recruit. Years later, I met and worked with Jon Luther, CEO and chairman of Dunkin' Donuts. Jon taught me many things, including the fundamentals of building a winning leadership team. Through a philanthropic event I got to know Bill Belichick, and now he is a friend and someone whose team-building and game-calling I study closely.

I ask questions of and study the best and most gifted recruiters out there. I want to know what they know and what they are thinking when they build a team. What are they looking for? What are they *not* looking for? What are the most important qualities in a recruit?

I also understand that in building a team—and this is the case when trying to be a success in many areas—you need to be aware of what you don't know, and then go about correcting that ignorance. You should never stop learning and asking questions.

What complicates the recruiting and talent development process is that a recruit, who might be the right one at one stage of the development of a corporation or mission, might not be a good fit at another stage. For example, it seemed that, depending on the assignment, or the status of war and peace, General George S. Patton was either the most valuable officer in the U.S. Army or a very problematic one.

Great recruiters have helped me to be able to teach and coach recruiting—and to be able to transmit to organizations the critical elements that need to be respected and observed if you are to get the most out of your draft selections.

Picking the right players requires considerable time and effort—and you can never be good enough at it.

Not Necessarily the Best Players—But the Right Ones

Among all the spoken lines and quotes that popular media and art has rendered and produced concerning the 1980 men's U.S. Olympic hockey team, perhaps the dialogue that most intrigues managers and coaches, and which they find most useful, is a conversation in the movie *Miracle* that takes place between U.S. team assistant coach Craig Patrick (played by Noah Emmerich) and head coach Herb Brooks (played by Kurt Russell).

It is early in the team tryouts in Colorado Springs and Patrick is looking over a roster of the names of the final 26 players (which eventually will be cut to 20), and with a tone of surprise he says to Herb, "You're missing some of the best players." And Herb responds,

"I'm not looking for the best players, Craig. I'm looking for the right ones."

I'm not looking for the best players, Craig. I'm looking for the right ones.

What does that mean? It means not building a *team of all-stars*—but an *all-star team*.

It means finding and training (as I will later explain, recruiting is an ongoing process) the people who offer your team the best chance for success. It means finding and bringing on board the people who fit with the *culture* of your group.

Day in and day out, in companies and in groups, there are very smart and able people who fail, who are fired, who are facing a dead-end at a company, or who figure out that they just aren't right for the place. What is interesting is that while one person at a company is on the way out, there is a person in the next office or over the divider in the next cubicle who, while not as smart or even as hardworking, is thriving in the enterprise.

One person is right for the culture—another isn't.

I often deliver a version of this message to audiences—especially if I am speaking to a group of people in a company that is undertaking a bold mission, or if it is a group that has been recently created from the merging of two companies: "You can be the brightest and most focused and hardest working person in the room, yet if you are not bought into the agenda or the mission of this organization, then you are not the type of person this organization needs to succeed."

It isn't a matter of who is best—but who is right for the job.

The 1980 U.S. Olympic hockey team was a collection of people who were right for the job.

It is an example of picking the right players.

Team Chemistry Is Essential

Team chemistry is a popular term, if not a popular notion. What I mean is that many people talk about team chemistry, and it is a nice sounding, inspirational phrase, but I think that the essence and guts of team chemistry are neither studied nor practiced in depth.

The first step in developing winning team chemistry is to select the players or employees who you will work with and train. You want talented and smart people, but you also want the people who will work best in and for your organization. You want people who will operate well together, and who complement one another. Sure, when you think of team chemistry on a macro level you are thinking team culture, but on a micro level you are thinking operations.

You also need to think ahead about what the game or the competitive environment will require of your team: different personnel, different combinations, and formations.

In sports, you have to be aware of that macro and micro thing when concocting winning solutions. Macro is the type of team you build and its overall chemistry. You think micro when you consider the personnel changes and adaptations required for different situations in a game. For example, in hockey, your "kill-the-penalty" line as opposed to your power-play line; in football, your goal-line defense compared against the defense you use when you are facing the opponent deep in its territory; in basketball, the lineup on the court you use when you are pressing compared against who you have on the floor when you are sitting back in a two-three zone.

What are the best personnel combinations? "Remember that on our team we had the Conehead Line. Buzzy, Pav, and Bah were not aliens from another planet, but definitely from a place far away, the Iron Range in Minnesota; it was a place that had its own form of hockey, a form that those three played together exceedingly well. I mentioned earlier that Iron Range hockey was "creative and explosive and unpredictable." It sure is. It is a style of hockey that doesn't betray anything early, especially offensively; its potential is deceptive—but it can go from 0 to 60 . . . make that 0 to 90 . . . in a few seconds."

ESPN reported of the Coneheads, "When the play looked most innocent, that's when the Coneheads were most dangerous."

Pavelich and Harrington and Schneider were best when they were together. So they were kept together. They were the only three who remained together on the same line throughout the Olympics.

Overall, what were the elements, the individual talents that were recruited to create the "Miracle on Ice" team? The team was weighted heavily with exceptional speed and skating; these were the qualities undergirding all of our play and success. We were fashioned and constructed to play on the bigger sheet of ice of international competition, and to be able to be compete with the jets and constant passing of the Soviets.

Speed was the essence of the Red Army Team's success. We had no chance if we did not have the necessary speed to counter this strength.

We also held on to some of the physical play that was the tradition of American and Canadian hockey. We absolutely would do some banging on the boards and keep our elbows out and check from end to end—but we were not a team of bruisers that could overwhelm you with muscles and strength. Because of our speed and nimbleness, we did not have to rely on an occasional bone-jarring leveling of an opponent to gain an advantage, but, rather, we knit together frequent hits and checks—not one of which by itself would make a highlight film—but which cumulatively took their toll.

You know, some 20 years after the Lake Placid games, I was at a rink in the Boston area and I was surprised to see there the great Soviet defenseman Vladimir Lutchenko, the "Bobby Orr of Soviet hockey." Vladimir, who won Olympic gold medals in 1972 and 1976 (and who was not on the 1980 Soviet Olympic team), was lightning-fast on skates. He was now working as the on-site pro at a rink that was owned by a Russian businessman. Vladimir and I became friends, and we coached youth teams and played in adult hockey leagues together.

When Vladimir talks about great Soviet players and the strength of the Soviet system, he doesn't talk long without mentioning speed and explosiveness. Those traits he repeats over and over.

Soviet speed and explosiveness enabled it to dominate international hockey for decades. U.S. speed and explosiveness enabled it to come out on top over two weeks in February in 1980.

Look for Those Who Will Dream Big—But Not Make Dreams Their Master

In his ode to ambition, *If*, Rudyard Kipling wrote, "If you can dream—and not make dreams your master."

Herb Brooks, whose favorite films included *Willy Wonka and the Chocolate Factory*, told the *Minneapolis Star-Tribune*, "You know, Willy Wonka said it best: We are the makers of dreams, the dreamers of dreams. We should be dreaming. We grew up as kids having dreams, but now we're too sophisticated as adults, as a nation. We stopped dreaming. We should always have dreams. I'm a dreamer."

Nothing great is achieved without big dreamers who have the work ethic, fortitude, gumption, and daring necessary to make their dreams happen. When you are building your team, be on the lookout for them.

Search for people who will dare to do great things, who will not be limited by convention, who have swagger and who are audacious, who believe in the impossible, and who are overly confident (and be aware that confidence is sometimes *quiet* confidence).

Cynics and doubters need not apply for greatness.

Look for people who can handle the heat. In athletics there are many big-time and exceptional practice players who wilt when it gets to the opening face-off, tap, kickoff, or pitch. To drill down even further, there are big-time game players, just not when the pressure is on and the score is tied and the seconds remaining are few. I say that you should build a team of gifted players who are all crunch-time certified.

Every player on our team had attitude and a fire to compete and prove himself. There is no secret that I earned a reputation for being vocal and cocky and having a lot of confidence. Yet, those qualities enabled me to get the most out of my natural gifts, and to be the best last line of defense for my teammates.

I was a dreamer from a young age. My attitude energized and nurtured me as I chased my dreams.

Peter Cappuccilli places the American flag on the shoulders of Jim following the gold-medal clinching win over Finland.
Credit: AP Images

If I didn't have that attitude I may have accepted what the college scouts originally thought—that I couldn't play big-tine college hockey. If I didn't have that attitude I may have fallen apart during the Olympics.

All my teammates had dreams—and all of them could handle the pressure.

I say that we were not a Dream Team but rather a *Team of Dreamers*.

There is a big difference between the two. And I don't think we will see such a team of dreamers again anytime soon.

Recruit the Dreamers Who Can Handle Defeat

There is a public relations professional who does a lot of work for me and Gold Medal Strategies. Among the work he does for me is to go over my speeches and make suggestions, and he also helps prepare my teamwork coaching seminars.

This guy is a big Abraham Lincoln fan. He studies Lincoln's life, what he wrote and what he said. I once asked my friend, "Why does Lincoln interest you so much?"

Among the qualities and elements of Lincoln's life, he said what he found most interesting and inspiring was that Lincoln knew a tremendous amount of despair and defeat, yet, even while it seemed Lincoln had a tough time shaking the despair, he surely didn't stay defeated. He bounced back—over and over.

Further—and this ties to the element of big dreams—it seemed that Abraham Lincoln had a sense of destiny, a feeling that it was in the cards for him to achieve something extraordinary and play an important role in shaping history. I guess when you are confident of that future then you can handle some setbacks and losses.

Look for a never-say-die spirit when building your team.

One of the more unheralded players on our team was Mark Wells. He was a guy who exemplified the not-accepting-defeat attitude—and being able to rebound from criticism—that defined our squad. Wells, the final player added to the roster that traveled to Lake Placid, was a center on the fourth line. At 5-8, he was not big for the position, especially since he would be relied on to check opposing scorers. Here was a guy that the experts deemed not good enough to play Junior hockey—but he made it at that level. He was told over and over he couldn't play major college hockey; he again proved the doubters wrong and did very well at Bowling Green. He surely couldn't play in the Olympics either, right?

For several months prior to the Olympics, he was a guy who dreamed of Olympic glory, yet it seemed he hadn't—and wouldn't—achieve his dream.

Wells didn't travel with the team when we barnstormed through the United States and Europe. He said he felt like an outsider—and I understand why. But when he got his chance he played and competed with as much zeal and intensity as anyone on our team. In the Russian game, he had the unenviable task of checking and shadowing Valery Kharlamov, among the fastest, most agile, and scary scorers in hockey history.

It should have been a mismatch, but not that night. Look at the tapes. What you will see is the kid who was told he wasn't good enough to play Junior hockey performing more than good enough to frustrate and throw off the game of one of the greatest players on earth.

The Best Recruiters Are Master Salesmen

What good is being able to find the right talent if you can't sell him or her on signing with your company? You need to be able sell your organization and its vision.

My career itself is part and parcel of the investment that companies make in being able to sell the future. I may be in the hire of an investment firm, and speaking to a get-together of its high net worth clients—and also in the crowd are people with a load of dough who are not a client of the firm, but, of course, the firm would very much like to be on its client roster. I might speak for a major distributor of, let's say, medical products—at an awards dinner for its top producing sales reps. Also in the audience are star independent reps who are not selling the distributor's products—yet whom they very much want to sell its products.

In these situations, my speech is a hybrid of motivational material and interesting anecdotes—and an exposé on the merits and strengths of the firm hosting the event.

Selling a company—whether to a prospective employee or to a client—is recruiting.

In his successful effort to lure John Sculley away from Pepsi, Apple CEO and co-founder Steve Jobs pitched Sculley with this line: "Do you want to spend the rest of your life selling sugared water or do you want a chance to change the world?" That is some good selling.

There are people in Hollywood—very well-paid people in Hollywood—whose almost exclusive job is to pitch movie ideas to studios. Now, mind you, these professionals are not the screenwriters, directors, or the producers—but sales people who take the concept and are responsible for selling it.

In the college athletic ranks, some of the most successful coaching staffs, in terms of wins and losses, aren't necessarily the best in terms of Xs and Os. They are, however, master recruiters. As I say over and over, it is tough to beat superior talent. It can be done—but it is a lot easier to win when your team has players who are faster, smarter, and stronger than the competition.

The strength of a school's academics will play—well, let's hope that they play—a prominent role in a recruit's decision. So, too, will a winning program in the sport for which the student-athlete is being courted; this is especially true if the winning tradition is current.

A smart recruiter knows how best to pitch the strengths of his or her institution.

But no matter how many national championships the program has won, or how many Nobel Prize winners have graduated from or taught at the school, the chances are that a masterful recruiting effort—sales effort—will be needed to get a highly-sought-after prep athlete to decide that your college or university is where he or she will attend.

When you recruit for your company, you need to be a master salesman. When making your pitch, you need to sell more than a paycheck and a benefits package—although of course in the real world that is important. You need to sell people on the concept that if they sign with you and choose to work for your company, then they will be part of something important.

I am a national spokesperson for the medical equipment manufacturer W.L. Gore and its Ultimate SAAAVE, a public affairs campaign that encourages those at risk for abdominal aortic aneurysm, or triple-A as it is commonly called, to get screened for the condition. My dad died from a triple-A that ruptured. W.L. Gore makes a device that is inserted in a minimally invasive procedure that repairs a triple-A and prevents it from rupturing.

My primary job with Ultimate SAAAVE is to get the word out through in-person and media appearances. But I also speak to doctors and Gore salespeople to rally and inspire their efforts. I always push the message that, day in and day out, they are not just making a living—they are saving lives. They are doing some of the most important work in society.

All honest labor is sacred and vital to a healthy society.

A top recruiter—a master salesman— describes the importance of the labor performed at his or her organization.

After all, you can make money selling sugared water—but how much better is it to make money while changing the world?

Recruit the Right Values and Right Character

Branch Rickey took on the most important recruiting assignment in sports history: finding and persuading the "right man" for the job of breaking the color barrier in Major League Baseball.

Rickey, the Brooklyn Dodgers president and general manager, needed to find and successfully recruit more than a talented athlete;

the greater need was to find and convince someone to come on board with the mental toughness, the strength of values, and the character necessary to withstand abuse and continue to do his job while not being incited to do or say anything that would jeopardize the opportunity to dismantle the color barrier forever. The "right man" for the job would have to, in the short term, bite his tongue and not lash out at the insults and derision.

Branch Rickey found the "right man" in Jackie Robinson.

When you are putting together your team, you need talent and skills and experience, but you also need people with the right values and character. Values and character are the bedrock of any team culture—whether it is a hockey team or construction company. Values and character need to be fairly consistent across your organization; indeed, having this consistency is essential to having a shared dream.

When Cone, a leading strategy and communications agency (with which I have worked), begins a brand-building and corporate identity assignment with a company, one of the first things it does is to get managers and execs together to assess what the values are of the organization.

"It can be a difficult process—and very emotional," says Cici Gordon, vice president of business development for Cone. "But if you don't have shared values then you aren't sure of who you are—and you don't have a common culture. Without identity and without culture, what is your story and what is your brand?"

In recruiting the 1980 U.S. Olympic hockey team, the values and character that Herb Brooks sought were those of mental toughness, confidence, pride in one's work—and a willingness to listen and learn, adopt a different type of play, and to give up and change a position or role for the betterment of the group. Actually, these are values and character traits that would be helpful for any team to have.

Take the case of Mark Johnson. Mark, or "Magic", as we called him, was one of the most effective and dangerous scorers on earth.

Herb wanted Mark on the team because of his physical abilities—his abilities to put the puck in the net, and to keep our opponents in a constant state of worry. Yet Herb also wanted Mark on the team because of his stalwart character and intensity.

Even many talented players would have given up chasing the puck with only a few seconds remaining in the first period of the Soviet game with our team down 2-1. Soviet goalie Vladislav Tretiak surely did; he allowed a careless rebound of Dave Christian's long slapshot. But Mark Johnson always played until the buzzer sounded, and he gathered the puck and put it past Tretiak with one second remaining in the period.

Herb recruited Mark Johnson for the physical skills and character that enabled him to score that vital tying goal.

When the character and values aren't right, then your team doesn't play right. You can get away with a mishmash of character traits and values within your team for awhile and win—or you can get away with it for the long term and eventually go on a losing streak—but for long-term success you need to have a team of players with the right values and of high character.

■ ■ ■

One of the best brand-builders on earth is Jon Luther, a mentor and a good friend of mine as well. Jon Luther is the executive chairman of Dunkin' Brands, whose two brands—Dunkin' Donuts and Baskin-Robbins—are both among the best-known and iconic brands in America.

From 2003 through 2006, Jon served as chief executive officer of Dunkin' Brands; he was named chairman in 2006. At the helm of Dunkin', Jon took, to use a Dunkin' inside term, a "dirty donut shop" that operated only in New England to markets across the country and, now, internationally.

Jon, who came to Dunkin' Brands after turning around Popeye's Chicken, selects his management team using a system he calls

Values-Based Leadership—a business philosophy and process that includes looking for the following seven values of character:

- Honesty—You can always recover from the truth.
- Integrity—Character shows when no one else is looking.
- Responsibility—Own the outcome, good or bad.
- Humility—It's about the team; never lose sight of those who helped you along the way, or those less fortunate in our communities.
- Fairness—Always do the right thing, especially when it's tough to do.
- Respectfulness—Give people their dignity; earn other's respect.
- Transparency—Show your thoughts without hesitation.

Jon uses these values in selecting his leadership team—and that leadership team uses these values in its own recruiting. Values-Based Leadership is the foundation of the phenomenal success of Dunkin' Brands.

■ ■ ■

I have learned at the elbow of some of the best recruiters from across many different sectors and industries. I have asked many questions. Reinforced and emphasized, over and over, is that winning is dependent upon people who work well together and who have common character traits and values. When they aren't in place then you have dysfunction.

I have actually developed a fairly keen ability to detect quickly within a group which people aren't right for winning and finding solutions. They may have been at one time, but they aren't now. This brings up another point: The person you recruited may have had the right character and values—but sometimes things change. It is a manager's job to help support the maintenance of the qualities needed for victory.

Recruit people with the right values and character—and build your organization around them.

Stick with the Plan—Own the Outcome

Sports coaches and organizational managers owe recruits mentorship and the resources necessary for success. You locate potential—and then you work with it. I was fortunate to have a goalie coach for my international hockey career who subscribed to this philosophy. His name was Warren Strelow, one of the best goalie coaches ever.

In the *Boys of Winter*, Wayne Coffey describes a component of this philosophy:

> Working with goaltenders is like building a house, Strelow believes. You begin with a solid foundation, with fundamentals such as balance, being square to the puck, knowing how to read and react to certain situations. When the foundation is in place, you build up from there. But underpinning everything is self-confidence and the ability to cope with good things and bad things with the same emotional stability.

Whether a recruit or draft pick succeeds has a lot to do with how that person is managed and coached. The job of a supervisor is to bring along talent. You owe professional development to people within your organization. Sometimes you will see the potential where others won't. Consider that Michelangelo sculpted his masterpiece *David* from a piece of marble that had been rejected by two other artisans because they considered it imperfect.

There is no better organization in training winners and leaders than the U.S. military. In talking with and asking questions of the men and women who have served in positions of leadership in the armed forces, I heard over and over how vital it is for leaders to stay invested in the development of the people under their command and direction. They know that a soldier can never be good enough, and that leaders are constantly teaching, directing, guiding, and inspiring.

■ ■ ■

New York Giants manager Leo Durocher stuck with the plan and owned the outcome of the decision to bring up from the minors a 20-year-old outfielder. Durocher was steadfast and committed, even though the young man was 1-for-25 at the plate since his Big League debut (albeit the one hit was a home run in his thirteenth plate appearance, and it came off of future Hall of Famer Warren Spahn). The player even asked Durocher to return him to the minors, saying that he felt he couldn't hit Major League pitching. Durocher said no, that he believed in him, and that as long as he was manager the kid had a place on the Giants.

Durocher knew what he was doing. The kid began to hit. The kid's name was Willie Mays.

Herb Brooks and Warren Strelow stayed with Jim Craig.

In the Olympics, in the first period against Germany, I let up two goals off of long slap shots. Herb told backup goalie Steve Janaszak to get ready. Herb wasn't sure he wanted to make this move but he thought ahead, and if I let up another goal, he wanted Steve to be warmed up and able to jump right in.

Herb told Warren that he was thinking of taking me out—and he wanted to know what Warren thought. Warren said, "No. He hasn't lost this game. We have to stay with him. He'll play through this and be a better goalie because of it."

I remained in net.

In any position of leadership and responsibility, whether you are a military officer, corporate executive, non-profit executive director, high school principal, college dean, or sports coach, you are going to face questions about your picks and selections. Sometimes, sure, the critics are right. But as I wrote earlier in this chapter, and I want to emphasize it again because it is so important, you have to give your personnel time and you are responsible for mentoring, teaching, and developing their talent.

Work at it and give your decision time to be proven correct—or proven wrong.

No matter—stick with the plan and own the outcome.

Beyond the Ice—Other Mentors and Coaches

Belichick

In 2008, on a Thursday late in May, I was in a car returning home from a speech I had delivered in the Catskills. I had a driver, so I was able to get some work done on the trip. I checked my voicemails; one I received was from my good friend Bill Belichick.

Bill is a big lacrosse fan, especially Johns Hopkins men's lacrosse, and in his voicemail he asked if I would deliver a pep talk to the Johns Hopkins team the day prior to its NCAA tournament semifinal against heavily favored Duke. The tournament that year was being held at Gillette Stadium, the home of the Patriots, and about 10 miles from my office. I called Bill back and told him I would be happy to do it. The Johns Hopkins—Duke game was in two days.

When I arrived at Gillette Stadium the next day to speak to the team, I was met by Berj Najarian, Director of Football/Head Coach Administration for the Patriots, and for all intents and purposes the right-hand man to Coach Belichick, and someone in whom Bill places great confidence. Bill was not there that day as he was down at his alma mater, Wesleyan University, to receive the honor of induction into the university's athletic hall of fame.

Berj showed me around, and we stopped by Bill's office. I took in the shelves of books, the mementos, and the memorabilia—and there I saw, on the wall facing Bill's desk, the framed photo of the 1980 U.S. Olympic hockey team's celebration on the ice following our victory over the Soviet Union.

Berj pointed to the photo and said, "Just so you know—that isn't there because you are here today. That is *always* there."

Needless to say, it brought me no small amount of happiness, and some pride, that one of history's greatest coaches and winners, and someone for whom I have tremendous admiration, places prominently and in direct line of sight from his workstation an image of our triumph in Lake Placid.

Among the many reasons I admire Bill Belichick is for his achievements as a recruiter and team-builder. These achievements are founded and dependent on his extraordinary work ethic, focus, love for the game, institutional intelligence, and God-given smarts. Of course, these are the qualities his father, Steve Belichick, a brilliant football coach, who was also passionate about the game, shared with, and passed along to Bill.

Bill had told me how much he admired the traits of our team, how he values and is inspired by the path we took to the podium, and that in coaching the Patriots, he has put to use the lessons of our success at Lake Placid. Still, to see that photo there, and to know that it is always there, well, that was special.

What the career of Bill Belichick teaches us is that recruiting and picking the right players requires a lot of *hard* work—and a lot of *smart* work. It requires strategy and analysis and foresight. And you can't do it alone. Similar to what Jon Luther does at Dunkin' Brands, Bill Belichick recruits the recruiters.

Belichick was named coach of the New England Patriots in 2000. He surrounded himself with a staff exceptional in its ability to evaluate what talent was needed to win—and how best to compete and obtain that talent. Among these staff members were player personnel director Scott Pioli, and long-time friend and genius football strategist, Ernie Adams, who was named Football Research Director. Two seasons later, Belichick brought in more smarts in defensive coordinator Romeo Crennel and offensive coordinator Charlie Weis, both of whom were fundamental to the Patriots winning the 2003 and 2004 Super Bowls.

Any comprehensive study of Coach Bill Belichick requires reading *The Education of a Coach* by David Halberstam. There will be other books written about Bill Belichick, yet it will be tough to write a better one than did Halberstam, a Pulitzer Prize-winning giant of American journalism and writing, who died in 2007 when a car in which he was a passenger crashed.

An area on which Halberstam focuses in the book is the working relationship between Belichick and Patriots team owner Bob Kraft, and how they agreed that being able to operate effectively with the NFL salary cap made all the difference in the world as to whether you build a winning franchise. A salary cap is just that—a limit on how much a team can pay for players. There are ways to get around it; for example, a "signing bonus" is not considered salary. But a bonus is also risky for owners because unlike salary money, signing bonus money is "guaranteed," whether the player performs like an all-star or gets cut.

With the salary cap, analysis and evaluation of potential is paramount. You are constantly looking for the hidden gem, the uncut diamond, the sleeper. You are always searching to purchase premium at a discount. Anyone who is in a position of hiring, whether in the private or public sector, knows the salary cap well.

And, especially if money is tight, you want to do what the New England Patriots did: draft Tom Brady in the sixth round.

Halberstam writes about the admiration that Kraft had for Belichick as an NFL recruiter and team builder:

> One of the things that impressed him in his early talks with Belichick, when the latter was an assistant head coach in New England, was that Belichick seemed to think much the same way, and could break the team down, player by player, and give a knowing estimate of the value received for each player. Belichick had come up with his own philosophy of how to operate in the current NFL; he seemed wary of throwing big money at available superstar players. A truly great player, one

who completely altered a given game, a Lawrence Taylor, he said, came along very rarely. The right model was to scout well, both in the draft and free agency, and create a team with a lot of good players, in effect a team with a significant amount of depth and as many interchangeable parts as possible.

Other teams were consumed with the need to sign as many superstars as possible. Not Bill Belichick and the Patriots. He built a team that had very good players—and some superstars—but there was more of an objective to work with the salary cap to draft and sign the components that worked best together, and which would deliver results in the short and long term.

■ ■ ■

The genius of Bill Belichick and his staff also resided in selling the fulfillment of being part of something great. They were able to do this because the players that were being pitched looked at the plan and understood it would work. They were being sold a quality product.

You wanted to play for the New England Patriots—even if you had to take a pay cut to do it. It says something that even after Tom Brady has quarterbacked New England to three Super Bowl wins, he receives a pay package from the club that places him in the middle of the pack in terms of what starting NFL quarterbacks earn. Brady agrees to this because he wants the team to have more money to pay other players.

In 2007, when megastar Randy Moss took a pay cut to be a Patriot, he told the media, "I think over the course of my career. I still have money in the bank. By me coming to an organization such as the New England Patriots, why would money be a factor?"

The Patriots won the franchise's first Super Bowl in 2002, upsetting the St. Louis Rams in New Orleans. New England went 9-7 the following year and missed the playoffs. But Belichick and Company were building and creating something special. They were—to use that term again—signing premium at a discount, and landing talent that other teams had not appraised properly, or who might not work in a system other than what was in place in New England.

Halberstam wrote that the Patriots were landing players that "tended to support the values that Belichick was trying to instill," and as they continued to land the right players for their system, the "players themselves were beginning to buy in and enforce a winning culture."

I do want to say here that professional football is big business. Bill Belichick and Robert Kraft are businessmen. And while the success of the Pats has been an immense feel-good for the region, it is also success that has often been established without a lot of sentimentality. Or if sentimentality is there, decisions and choices have to be made despite it.

The Pats have released players who did not agree to taking less money—and they have driven hard agreements in negotiations with athletes that the Pats were interested in signing. Due to money, or other reasons that a player no longer worked for the system, New England has said bye to fan favorites such as quarterback Drew Bledsoe and defensive back Lawyer Milloy.

Indeed, the Patriots have received criticism for what many felt was stinginess. Late in the 2003 preseason, when Milloy would not take a pay cut, New England released him. The Pats immediately took the heat for the decision. It got hotter when the Patriots played at Buffalo the first game of the season and lost 31-0 to a Bills team that had Milloy starting in the secondary.

Maybe, though, Belichick and company knew what they were doing. The season ended better than it began—with the Pats beating the Carolina Panthers to win their second Super Bowl in two years. The following year, the Patriots went on to make it back-to-back Super Bowl wins, downing the Philadelphia Eagles.

Bill Belichick is a winner. I have learned from his example. You can too.

By the way, that lacrosse game, the one between Johns Hopkins and Duke? Well, Johns Hopkins knocked off Duke in what is considered one of the biggest upsets in recent collegiate lacrosse history.

Great Teams Are the Product of Picking the Right Players Chapter Recap

- **Team Chemistry Is Essential:** Recruit individuals who will work and operate effectively together—and who will complement one another. The whole is greater than the sum of its parts.
- **Look for Those Who Will Dream Big—But Not Make Dreams Their Master:** Build a team of people who dream big—but who also understand and are committed to the work and risks necessary to achieve dreams.
- **The Best Recruiters Are Master Salesmen:** You need to be able to sell and get people to buy in to your vision.
- **Recruit the Right Values and Right Character:** All the talent in the world can be undermined by competing values and lack of character within an organization. Recruit people who share the right values and right character.
- **Stick with the Plan—Own the Outcome:** Work with your draft picks—train them. That is your responsibility. However it turns out, you are accountable for the choice you made.

Great Teams Are the Product of Picking the Right Players & Chapter Recap

6

Great Teams Have a Real or Invented Enemy

A ndy Grove always looks for the enemy.

Grove, an immigrant from Hungary, was one of the first employees of Intel, and he rose to become its top executive. He is credited with stewarding Intel to become one of the most successful high-tech companies in the world. *Time Magazine* named Grove its "Man of the Year" for 1997. In 2006, Grove gave $26 million to his alma mater, City College of New York.

Grove authored a business book titled *Only the Paranoid Survive*. Grove has written, "I believe that the prime responsibility of a manager is to guard constantly against other people's attacks and to inculcate this guardian attitude in the people under his or her management."

I agree totally with Andy Grove. When I speak to groups, when I coach teamwork, I strongly emphasize the importance of having enemies—real or invented—and being on guard against their destructive potential. If you don't see an enemy out there, then you are in trouble.

I speak to financial planners and advisors from many different companies. I like to challenge them—put them on guard. As a guy in his early 50s, with a family, and someone who works hard and is fortunate to make a good living, I am a prime business target for financial advisors. I can make them money. I receive calls and emails frequently from people who want to advise and guide my savings and investments. I tell the groups to which I speak about the frequent contact I receive. I also tell them that it is impossible for any investor or advisor to be too good when handling the finances of my family.

"So, everyone out there, think of your clients—think of your top clients," I say to the advisors. "Do you think you are the only advisor that they have? Oh, you don't think, you know you are. Well, good for you. You are sure of that, right?"

I get them thinking—and then I continue:

"Yeah, maybe you are correct—that client or this client only works with you. But is this the way it will continue? Who called them yesterday? Today? Or who will call them tomorrow? Will someone, a friend or business colleague, whom they trust greatly suggest another advisor?"

One thing for certain, most high-net-worth people work with more than one advisor. Of course, every client, whether she or he doesn't have much to invest, or whether there is a mountain of money there to be handled, should be treated with the same interest and care. But I need to be realistic here—and if I want to make the lesson urgent, I focus on the big-money people who could go away.

I'm putting the enemy on their radar screen. Being a bit paranoid helps in recognizing the enemy, or in conjuring one up.

Identify and Fixate on a Common Enemy

You have to hand it to Vladislav Tretiak for telling the truth. After the 1980 Winter Olympics, he admitted that, as the games approached, he and his teammates didn't consider the U.S. to be viable competition—not a true enemy. In fact, he said the U.S. "never really counted" as an opponent.

A few days prior to the start of the Lake Placid games, we played the Soviets at Madison Square Garden in an exhibition—a sort of final tune up. We got crushed, 10-3. And it wasn't as close as the score might suggest. We could do nothing. They could do everything.

That thrashing did us more good than it did the Soviets. I've always said that you learn more from defeat than victory.

You see, if the Soviets didn't take us very seriously prior to the game at Madison Square Garden, they didn't take us seriously at all after it. When they took to the ice against us in the Olympic medal round, they had their guard down, they were not focused, and did not appreciate what they were up against.

They did not think we were a very good team, which we were. The previous time we played them, we were intimidated and we had an off-night. But this wouldn't be the case in the game we played on Friday evening, February 22, 1980.

Think of our advantage. The whooping we received at Madison Square Garden was a downer for sure. But the experience also relieved us of some awe. We got pounded, yes, but we now figured things couldn't get any worse. In fact, we had collectively resolved that if we met up with the Red Army Team in Lake Placid, no matter the final score, we would not play it as a group of star-struck and intimidated schoolboys, or as merely a foil and stepping stone for the Soviets, but as a team of overachieving young men who were going to make them work across every inch of ice. We were not going to get—to use a modern term—"punked" at Lake Placid.

Several years after our historic upset of the Red Army Team, its coach Viktor Tikhonov told *Boys of Winter* author Wayne Coffey that the game at Madison Square Garden had set his team up for defeat.

"No matter what we tried we could not get that 10-3 game out of the players' minds," said Tikhonov. "The players told me it would be no problem. It turned out to be a very big problem."

We left New York City with an enemy. The Soviets left with reaffirmation of them inevitably winning a fifth consecutive gold medal.

Tikhonov was right about the overconfidence factor. Then again, after the game, there was a lot of finger pointing among the Soviet players and coaches and across society back in their homeland.

A big strategic question was whether Tikhonov should have yanked goaltender Vladislav Tretiak after the first period. Several years into his retirement, Tretiak, who won Olympic gold in 1972 and 1976, and would win a third in Sarajevo in 1984, reflected on the decision to bench him, saying, "I would have had four gold medals if not for Tikhonov's bad judgement."

■ ■ ■

The Soviets had more talent than we did. They had better skills and were stronger and faster. But their talent advantage was not so strong that they could afford to look past us and treat us lightly. Yet, at Lake Placid they did just that—and in the preliminary round they took other teams lightly as well. They had played a bit lackluster against Finland and Canada, falling behind each team before firing up the jets and coming back to win.

The Soviets had become so accustomed and used to winning that they no longer had an enemy.

"They're not into it; for some reason the Russians are off their game," said Herb. "They're ready to slit their own throats. All we have to do is give them the knife."

We had the knife, and it had been kept sharp.

Of course, our big advantage is that this wasn't a "best of three" or "best of five" series. It was only one game. By the time the Soviets had figured out that they were playing against an enemy, it might be too late for them.

In the locker room before the game, Herb spoke those famous words—words that reflected on the need that we only needed to catch them sleeping and unaware on one night:

One game. If we played 'em 10 times, they might win nine.
But not this game, not tonight. Tonight we skate with them.
Tonight we stay with them. And we shut them down *because*

we can! Tonight WE are the greatest hockey team in
the world.

Were we the greatest hockey team in the world? For one
night we were.

■ ■ ■

Our competition at Lake Placid was not our only enemy. We had
an internal enemy—and not the type of internal enemy I will talk
about later in this chapter. That internal enemy was our coach. That's
right, the man without whom our gold medal victory would not have
happened.

This is exactly as Herb Brooks wanted it. I'll explain.

After the tournament in Colorado Springs, the squad was down
to 26 players from which the final 20 would be selected. And though
we were only about six months out from our first Olympic game,
we still did not have the enemy or enemies in sight that we needed
in order to reach our potential.

When I played for Boston University our archenemy was down
the street from us—literally. Even though BU and Boston College
were located in different communities—BU in Boston and BC in
Newton—Commonwealth Avenue connected both our campuses.
BC helped BU and me operate at peak efficiency. But, as I looked
toward Lake Placid, focusing on BC as an enemy was not going to
do the team or me much good. Getting fired up to play Providence
College or Northeastern University or Harvard University, all local
rivals to BU, also was not what was needed now.

University of Minnesota guys may not have very much liked the
University of Minnesota-Duluth guys—and Mark Johnson, who
played for the University of Wisconsin, had no love lost for either
of those schools, but these rivalries and competitive fires contained
powerful emotion and energy that needed to be rechanneled and
redirected.

Soon we had the focus on where we would rechannel and redirect that emotion and energy—and it was focused on Herb Brooks. We were all bought in. He rode us, ticked us off, challenged us, and rarely let up. We got angry and established together that he was our enemy, and, together, we were going to prove his criticism of us wrong.

Having Herb as the common enemy—again, his plan all along—required us to stop squabbling among ourselves and to ditch the regional rivalries.

The plan, of course, worked.

In the locker room after we beat Finland, I shouted at Herb—now with a smile—what all my teammates were feeling: "I showed you!" Herb said back to me, "You sure did, Jimmy."

In truth, every single player on that team showed Herb.

Plan, Prepare, and Execute

Winning at Lake Placid was the result of a lot of hard and smart work—and a lot of hard and smart planning and preparation. It was also about game day execution.

In sports, if a team has talent that is considerably better talent than its opponent, and gives the same effort, or close to the same effort, of its opponent, then the team with more talent will almost always win—no matter how excellent its opponent is tactically and strategically.

The U.S. was a very talented hockey team. As talented as the Soviets or the Czechs? Probably not. But we were not far behind. And I believe we had better talent than all the other teams in the tournament. In fact, we were so close in talent to the Soviets that if we played an almost flawless tactical and strategic game—and we played that game on a night the Soviets recognized too late what they were up against—then it could be enough to achieve the upset.

For the most part, international hockey at the time had two camps of tactics and play—there was the U.S. and Canadian camp which emphasized a bruising, physical, dump the puck and chase it form, and there was the European and Soviet camp which, partially because the playing surface was larger overseas, emphasized speed, constant circling and weaving, and frequent and precise passing.

Olympic competition was played on the same size rink on which the Europeans and Soviets regularly competed, so those teams had an advantage in the big tournament every four years. But no matter whether the game was played over here on our ice or over there on their ice, the Soviet form of hockey was successful. Yet into the late 1970s, neither the United States nor Canada had showed much desire to change their style of play even though the Soviets had been dominant in international competition for 20 years, including winning four straight Olympic gold medals.

Then there was the conditioning factor. The Soviets were always the best conditioned, the strongest, and the players with the freshest legs as the clock wound down. They could enter the third period a goal or two behind and remain confident in winning. It was just a matter of releasing fuel reserves and igniting afterburners—energy not available to the competition—and the Russians could drop three or four goals on you in 10 minutes.

Superior conditioning enabled those come from behind victories against the Finns and Canadians that I mentioned earlier. In both those games, the Russians looked to be on the ropes. Each time, though, they got off those ropes and fought to a win. First it was the Finns, who were up 2-1, with five minutes left. It took the Russians a minute and 19 seconds to score three goals. Final score: 4-2. Two days later, Canada, up 3-1 on the Soviets with less than a minute to go in the second period, had a clean look at a chance to make it 4-1, but missed. Damn if the Russians didn't score with 13 seconds remaining to the break. About two minutes after the puck dropped to start the third period, the Soviets had the lead, 4-3. Canada tied the game—but the Red Army Team scored two more goals to win, 6-4.

How could anyone beat these guys? Could it be done?

What Herb Brooks knew we needed to do in order to be competitive in the Olympics was to change our style of play and shake things up. He wanted to coach a team that played a hybrid—a revolutionary marriage of physical, dump-and-chase, and the European-Soviet model. "Throw their game back at them," said Herb. We would value possession of the puck and try to knock the Soviets off their game with our hard hitting and forechecking.

We would also upend history, in that we would be the fittest team on the ice; yes, fitter even than the Soviets. Getting there would require six months of Spartan training and practice, including types of training U.S. amateur squads had not traditionally done: weight training and plyometrics. Within that six-month period, over the five month stretch from early September through early February, we played 61 games at home and abroad.

We were prepared.

As a goalie, facing the Soviets was surely a different experience than playing against the Canadians, and different from playing against any other team as well. For example, the Canadians and West Germans would wind-up and shoot from anywhere, even if it wasn't a high-percentage shot. Canadian and West German teams shot the puck a lot. In all of international hockey, only the Czechs came close to the Russians in terms of discretion and being choosy in shooting the puck. Soviet teams would not take many shots—and you would rarely face a long slap shot delivered from anyone wearing one of those CCCP red sweaters—but, the shots that were taken were well planned, well set up, and were loaded with potential to turn on a red light. When the Soviets were on a rush it was a clinic in rapid-paced artistry: a pass ... and then a pass ... and then a pass ... and then a shot on net from 20 or 15 or 10 feet.

In the book *One Goal*, John Powers and Arthur Kaminsky described a "textbook" Soviet goal as "three touch passes and a 15-foot wrist shot up high."

If you look at and study the U.S.-Soviet game, you will see how strategy and conditioning played out. We played the game that we were trained to play, if not flawlessly, then very close to flawlessly. We were where we needed to be at the end of two periods—just a goal down and within striking distance. My teammates made smart decisions on both ends of the ice, and had checked the Soviets from end to end and side to side. In the final period, Mark Johnson scored, and then with 10 minutes remaining, Mike Eruzione delivered the "shot heard 'round the world." We were up, 4-3.

ABC TV announcer Al Michaels said, "Now we have bedlam." We were also a long way from the final buzzer against the most dangerous team on earth.

Think about how many teams have come close to a monumental upset, how many companies have been on the brink of doing something great, only to have the wheels come off the bus. The homestretch is gut-check time. A mistake that many organizations make, whether in sports or another sector, is to stop competing when ahead and there is a chance to close the door. They get defensive, go into a shell, and hope and pray that they will make it to 00:00 on the clock still ahead.

Were we going to do a Finland and Canada and shut down and let victory slip away?

Not a chance. If we lost, it would not be because we choked, held back, and stopped bringing it. We were going to keep thinking, playing our game, and making decisions that would help us win; we were not going to play just not to lose. There is an often-played and widely-seen video image of Herb, in the final minutes of the game. He is walking behind the players seated on the bench and saying calmly and assertively, over and over, "Play your game . . . play your game."

Against the Russians, we would play four lines against their three. And each of our shifts was to be no longer than 40 seconds. Herb reasoned correctly that this would help limit our fatigue. Our team physician, Dr. Nagobads, was responsible for the stop watch and maintaining the 40-second limit. He later joked that he didn't see much of the Miracle on Ice game because he was watching a clock all night.

The frequent shift changes confused and unnerved the Soviets. As Wayne Coffey recounted in the *Boys of Winter*, "On one comparatively long Russian shift, center Vladimir Petrov had a face-off with Johnson, another with Broten, and a third with Pavelich. He knew Nagobads from various international competitions. He caught the doctor's eye and asked in Russian, "*Shto to koy?*" (What is going on?)

"*Sprashike washe teneru*" (Ask your coach), replied Nagobads.

I wasn't part of any line change, but I needed to do my job until the final second expired—and I needed to keep thinking how to best help my teammates win. Early in the game, I tied up the puck in order to interrupt the flow of the Red Army team and minimize its explosive power. But, as the game progressed, I sensed that our advantage in conditioning and our frequent shift changes had the Russians gasping more than we were. So I adjusted. Now when I stopped a shot and was able to get a hold of the puck, I put it right back into play, preventing our opponents from getting a breather—and also keeping the clock ticking.

About that clock. Man, oh man, I have never seen a clock tick more slowly in my life.

What was also vital to our success that evening was that the Soviet players and the Soviet team did things that Soviet players and Soviet teams didn't normally do. Vladislav Tretiak didn't usually allow for a dangerous rebound on a shot he could have covered; but he did just that, and allowed Mark Johnson to tuck the puck past him to tie the game at 2-2 with a second left in the first period. Soviet players didn't quarrel among themselves on the ice—but, as the game went on, that happened as well. And the Soviets did not dump the puck and chase it—yet against us they did.

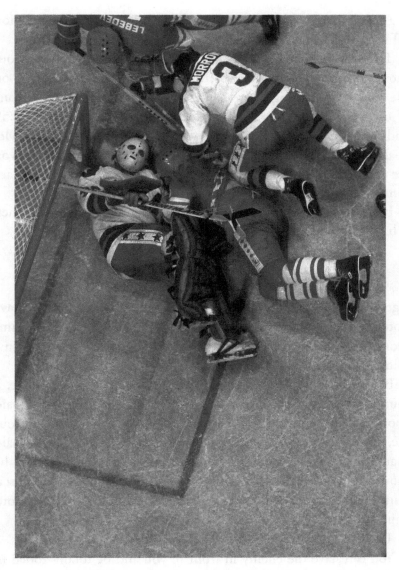

Scary moment. Late in the second period, Jim is briefly knocked out after a collision with a Soviet forward. Within a couple of minutes, though, Jim shakes off the grogginess and is back frustrating the Russians.

Credit: Photographer: Focus/On Sport/Getty Images

A combination of our strategy and fitness threw the Soviet Union off its customs and tendencies.

The way in which the final minute, final seconds, played out provided a bit of drama and commentary on the entire game—on the notion that things were a bit upside down that night. None of us could believe it when the clock got to 1:00 and then 00:59 and 00:58 ... and as time continued to tick away ... the Soviet goaltender Myshkin remained in net. It was Hockey 101: When you are down a goal in the final minute you pull your goalie and replace him with an extra scorer. But Myshkin went nowhere.

It was as if the Soviets had never been in this position, and when it happened, they did not know how to respond.

Be Ready for Anything—Respect Your Opponent

I grew up one town over from the city of Brockton, which I have noted is the hometown of undefeated heavyweight boxing champion Rocky Marciano and the adopted hometown of the long-time middleweight boxing champion, Marvelous Marvin Hagler.

Boxers need to be as focused on the enemy as any athlete. I found something interesting and very insightful that Hagler said about a fight in which he had his opponent hurt and in trouble, and was in the process of finishing him off. Hagler said that, yes, he would show no mercy and end the fight, but, as he moved in for the KO, he could not abandon caution and discipline because, as Hagler reflected, "a wounded animal is a dangerous animal."

There is a lesson here—one that transcends the boxing ring.

You can have the enemy in front of you and be totally zoned in on beating him or it. But in your quest you can never lose sight of, nor respect for, the potential and threat that the enemy poses to you.

Understand, as well, that there are enemies you don't see, but who are positioning themselves to enter your arena. Always be on guard for new entrants into the marketplace. In business there is the start-up, but there are also the established companies in another industry that might launch a division or another company that could compete against you.

As a competitive person, no matter the area of my life, I am intrigued and enjoy following the brutally competitive mobile and networked communications industries. They change so fast and attract so many of the gifted minds and driven souls that an enemy—a new company, a new technology, a new way of doing things—is about to run you over even if you never saw it on the long-off horizon.

You have to bring the "A game" every day, every time out, against every opponent. You'll recall the famous pre-Olympic game we played in Oslo against the Norwegian national team, a team not nearly as talented as us—a team of journeymen and guys who held day jobs outside of hockey—yet they managed to tie us. Herb was furious, as he should have been. We didn't respect the opponent. So after the game ended, he kept us on the ice and skated and skated and skated us.

We played the Norwegians the next day and beat them 9-0.

It was all a matter of respect and focus and effort.

The Enemies Within

When I was competing in hockey, I studied opponents exhaustively. I needed to know, inside and out, their strengths and weaknesses, their tendencies—and how the conditions of a game could affect those qualities and traits.

While I had some helpful genetics, what also enabled me to perform well in goal was that I worked hard to develop my physical and cognitive skills. In terms of the gray matter, did I have natural instincts that supported my ability to defend the net? Perhaps. But any smarts I used to my advantage on the ice were mostly acquired through study and observation.

In the business world, I continue to study and observe—and I think that I have cultivated a sensitivity and ability to quickly size up and evaluate personnel. It is said that the art of politics is to be able to figure out in a short time who is with you and who is against you—and who is undecided, and who can be persuaded. I have a bit of the politician in me.

Many times, while preparing for a speech, a manager will tell me that among the people I will be addressing are some that are not playing team and who are not onboard with the program. My job is to help recruit these people to play team and get on board—but oftentimes both the manager and I understand that it will be next to impossible to get cynics and doubters to buy in; more realistically, my job is to persuade them, through subtle and artful messaging, that the opportunity for them is elsewhere, with another company, on another team.

Now, I am not saying here that someone who isn't on board with your game plan is intentionally your enemy and is plotting to undermine and hurt your business—but the fact is that people who are not sharing in the dream support and nurture an internal mechanism that is not running right and efficiently. Lack of efficiency and lack of accountability are enemies of the organization. You need to be on guard for this and fix the problem.

Enemies within take on many forms.

Laziness is an enemy. Complacency is an enemy. Arrogance is an enemy. Overconfidence is an enemy. Jealousy is an enemy. Greed is an enemy (no matter what Gordon Gekko says). Ignorance is an enemy. Disorganization is an enemy. Lack of preparation is an enemy.

All of these negative traits are also negative energy. If you are a manager or coach or the head of a department, it is your job to recruit and train to prevent the enemy from within. Sometimes, of course, the enemy arises anyway—and then you need to manage and resolve the matter. If you don't do your job, then you are as much to blame for the problem as are the people within who are arrogant or not sufficiently up to date on a business practice, or a change in the market place, or who have become too comfortable and are not putting in the necessary time and effort to win, or who are so envious of the achievement of others that they are mouthing off and creating a problem.

You need to face the enemy—whether it is inside or outside of your group.

No matter if it is running my own company, or speaking for or coaching another company, or even if I am coaching a youth sports team, I prepare fully and give it my all—and that effort includes being on guard and heading off and eliminating the enemy from within.

A few years ago I was volunteering as a coach for a youth hockey team. I had a young man on the squad who was talented and had spirit, but he also didn't want to work and he copped a whole lot of attitude. I talked with him and I explained how he wasn't helping either his teammates or himself, and that he was actually hurting both. I related to him stories of athletes who had loads of potential, but who never reached their potential because they didn't care and weren't motivated and gave off negative energy. I told him that I didn't want to commit more time to working with him if he didn't change and become a team player. It wouldn't be fair to the other players.

I wouldn't have been doing my job as a coach if I didn't do this—for I would not have been dealing with and trying to remove an enemy from within our group. Now I am not saying the player was an enemy, but most certainly what was an enemy was his conduct that disrupted and undermined our team and prevented him from becoming the person and player I knew he could be. I also talked to the player's dad. I told him what was going on and the problems that had been created. I said that, unless his son started caring and working as a member of the team, I didn't want him playing and I didn't want to work with him. But if the athlete changed his tune and wanted to be a member of the team, then we would move forward. I suggested that father and son have a "Come to Jesus" meeting and talk this thing over.

The young man turned things around—thankfully. And it was partly my responsibility to try to make that happen.

You Take on the Enemy Together

Members of great teams come together to confront the enemy. Having that enemy helps you break down differences and overcome what divides you; it rallies the best in people, synthesizes it, and makes the total stronger than the sum of its parts.

If you focus together on the enemy, you are better prepared to win and achieve gold.

As essential as any component was to our team's success, was our extraordinary devotion to one another and the camaraderie we shared. Members of great teams care for one another. They are fervently committed to one another.

Ask anyone who is serving or who has served in the military about the importance of coordinated teamwork.

I was moved by a scene in the movie *Gladiator*, when the former military general, Maximus, and the other gladiators are in the arena; they are armed and will be forced to play a role in the re-creation of a great battle. Their adversaries will soon be coming through gates. It is a win-or-die situation.

"Anyone here been in the army?" Maximus asks the men around him.

A gladiator says yes and tells Maximus that he served under him in a particular battle.

Maximus says to the gladiator, "You can help me. Whatever comes out of these gates, we've got a better chance of survival if we work together. Do you understand? If we stay together we survive."

If we stay together we survive.

You take on the enemy together.

Beyond the Ice—Other Mentors and Coaches

Harold Connolly knew his enemy—and he fixated on him.

Connolly, born in 1931, came into this world with severe nerve damage to his left arm, a condition that would prevent the arm from ever developing properly. He grew up in the Boston neighborhood of Brighton. As a teenager he lifted weights to try to strengthen the arm. At Brighton High School he played football and also competed in the weight events for the school's track and field team. As well, while lifting weights or playing sports, he managed to break his left arm several times, injuries that caused further withering of the limb.

Connolly went on to nearby Boston College, attending without an athletic scholarship. He did not let his infirmity prevent him from taking up the weight throws at BC. There he was introduced to the hammer throw his senior year. He showed immediate and high-level promise in the event. After graduating from BC in 1953, he continued to train and compete and was soon the best hammer thrower in the United States.

After throwing the hammer for only two years and with his left arm about two-thirds the size of his right, Connolly became a force internationally in the event. He set his sights on the 1956 Olympic Games in Melbourne. To motivate and keep his focus, he pasted to the visor of his car a photo of Mikhail Krivonosov, the world record holder from the Soviet Union. Connolly would drive to and from practice, and to and from everywhere else, and would take a peek at the enemy, at Mikhail Krivonosov.

Fixating on the Soviets—the best in the world—as the Olympics approach. I've been there.

Connolly made the U.S. Olympic team, and about three weeks prior to the Melbourne games, at a meet in Los Angeles, he broke Krivonosov's world record. That didn't deter Krivonosov's teammates from preparing a victory cake that they would present to him after he won the gold medal. Into the fifth round of the hammer competition at Melbourne, it looked like Krivonosov would receive that cake. Connolly was actually in third place, trailing two Soviets—Anatoly Samotsvetov, who was in second place, and Krivonosov who was in first place with an Olympic record throw of 206'8".

Connolly wasn't done, though. On his fifth throw, he set an Olympic record with a distance of 207'3". The throw held up for the gold. Silver medal winner Krivonosov, gracious and a gentleman, presented "his" victory cake to Harold Connolly.

Harold Connolly knew his enemy. The very image of that enemy helped Connolly to the top of the victory podium at the 1956 Olympic Games in Melbourne.

Great Teams Have a Real or Invented Enemy—Chapter Recap

- **Identify and Fixate on a Common Enemy:** Identifying and fixating on a common enemy involves everyone on the team.
- **Plan, Prepare, and Execute:** Having an enemy does you no good if you are not preparing to defeat it—and if you are not able to get the job done when you are in the arena.
- **Be Ready for Anything—Respect Your Opponent:** Don't do a Soviet Union at Lake Placid. Anticipate new competition. Remember—"a wounded animal is a dangerous animal."
- **The Enemies Within:** Recognize and deal with problems in your own house.
- **You Take on the Enemy Together:** You prepare as a team and you compete as a team. Remember Maximus: "If we stay together we survive."

7

Great Teams Stay Young in Spirit and Outlook

You can't help getting older, but you don't have to get old.

—GEORGE BURNS

O n Sunday, February 14, 1980, our team took things to a new level when in our second game of the Olympics we beat Czechoslovakia, 7-3. Remember, we had come off an emotional final minute tie against Sweden on Friday. We were not expected to beat the Czechs—a team that many smart hockey people thought would take silver at Lake Placid and, maybe, even challenge the Soviets for gold. So, when we not only knocked off Czechoslovakia but actually soundly beat the team, we were not skating under the radar anymore. The U.S. was a very good hockey squad and we proved it.

Our third game was against Norway, a team that we were expected to beat—perhaps easily. Would we have a letdown, though, after the big win over the Czechs? We didn't play well early in the game. I let in a goal and we were losing 1-0 heading into the first intermission. We were playing stilted and nervous, in a sort of play-not-to-lose rather than play-to-win mode. We were sitting in the locker room and Herb had not come in yet. We were a bit down; we weren't getting the job done. Dave Silk tried to pump everybody up and he suggested that we all start saying positive things to, and be supportive of, one another. I remember what happened next—and *Sports Illustrated* actually reported it in a story. No one talked for a moment or two and my teammates kind of just looked at one another. Then came the chatter. From the *Sports Illustrated* story:

"'Eric, your hair looks marvelous.'

"'Phil, that's a wonderful job of taping your shin pads.'

"'Jimmy, your eyes are a lovely shade of blue.'

As Mike Eruzione noted later, 'We may be young but we're immature.'"

The youthful and immature banter eased things up; we started laughing and it helped us relax. Herb came in and told us we were a better team than Norway and just to play our game—and play it at full tilt. We came out of the locker room and dominated the remainder of the game and won, 5-1.

Joking, fun, and being kids were our MO—it helped us deal with the pressure heaped on us. It made us stronger. In September 1979, the team was on a sort-of barnstorming tour through Europe, playing games against European national teams and clubs. The tour was about preparing for and getting accustomed to the quality of competition we would face at Lake Placid; it was also about putting us in a situation in which the players would be forced to bond—as well as giving us breathing space from the U.S. media, administrators, organizers of American amateur hockey, and NHL coaches and scouts.

We were in Norway and taking a train from Oslo to Lillehammer. It was one of those sleeper trains with tight quarters and three-tiered bunk beds. Mark Wells, Ken Morrow, and I were figuring out the arrangements for one of the beds—and suddenly it hit me: the episode from *The Three Stooges* (remember I was born in 1957) called "Pain in the Pullman" when Moe, Larry, and Curley and their pet monkey are on a train with a traveling troupe of actors and entertainers that puts on shows. In that episode, the Stooges, without permission, are in the suite of the star of the show. The star discovers them and starts yelling for a Mr. Johnson, who is the show manager. He is yelling in this loud and deep voice, "Johnsonnn... Johnsonnn!" Mr. Johnson shows up and angrily boots the Stooges from the suite. Then the monkey gets loose and creates havoc. More hilarity ensues when the Stooges can't figure out how to get into the bunk bed—that looked a lot like the bunk beds on the train in Norway we were on—and that prompted my recall.

Yep, I couldn't help myself and I said to Kenny, "Hey, Kenny, you remember that Stooges episode on the train with the monkey—and that guy was yelling 'Johnsonnn ... Johnsonnn'? Kenny started laughing and says, "I sure do." Then I grabbed a small bag that Mark had and I tossed it to Ken, and I'm shouting, "Johnsonnn . . . Johnsonnn !" Wellsy tries to snatch the bag from Ken—but Ken throws it back to me while saying, "Johnsonnn . . . Johnsonnn." This goes on for about 20 seconds or so—Ken and I keeping the bag away from Mark as we bellowed, "Johnsonnn." We finally let up and gave the bag back to Mark.

We figured out bunk assignments: Mark got the bottom bunk, I took the middle bunk, and Ken took the top bunk. So we all lie down and try to get some sleep. Within a minute or two, Ken, who is 6'-4", tried to sit up and he smacked his head on the ceiling of the train car and he let out a yelp of pain and frustration.

Both Mark and I started laughing and were chirping, "Johnsonnn . . . Johnsonnn." Kenny, who minutes before thought this Three Stooges dialogue was hilarious—found none of it funny now.

Kenny Morrow had not heard the last of "Johnsonnn."

It wasn't long after Lake Placid, and the Atlanta Flames had a game at the Nassau Coliseum against the New York Islanders, for whom Kenny was playing his inaugural and starring role in what would be four consecutive seasons in which he, and the Islanders, won the Stanley Cup. The action had started and Kenny was on the blue line and the Flames were on the attack; the puck skittered toward the boards and the bench where I was located. Kenny moved in and I yelled, "Johnsonnn." Kenny kind of blinked, lost concentration, and the puck and our forward got past him. Kenny turned to me and muttered some choice words and turned to catch up to the play.

The free spirit and fun-loving mentality of the 1980 U.S. Olympic hockey team was an advantage for us. We were the youngest team in terms of age in the Olympic tournament—and we embraced it.

Herb said of us—"They're so young they still believe in Santa Claus."

If we sought to minimize the quality of our youth and prepare and play like a more mature version of ourselves—in other words, something we weren't—then I doubt we could have won it all. We laughed and we joked and we were feisty. When we scored, everyone came off the bench and engaged in a communal man-hug. We were kids. Energy and blissful ignorance enabled us to believe in things we had no right to believe in.

Even the ever-serious Herb Brooks—the one with the eyes that bore through you and the stare that could chill your soul—knew that kid-like fun, laughter, and frivolity, when strategically enlisted and introduced, can help make success possible. As we continued our winning through the Olympics, and more and more people began to pay attention to us, we became the newest darlings of America. As that historic showdown with the Soviet Union became imminent, Herb introduced levity to our preparation. He told us that the great Soviet wing, Boris Mikhailov, looked like Stan Laurel of the comedy team Laurel and Hardy. "You can beat Stan Laurel, can't you?" Herb asked us.

Remember that one of Herb's favorite movies was *Willy Wonka & the Chocolate Factory*.

Staying young in spirit and outlook is a quality of teams that do great things. When you get old your dreams can die and you can become complacent and satisfied with just good enough. That is a prescription for mediocrity and stunted growth.

When I do round tables with companies and other types of groups, I can frequently hone in quickly and accurately identify people within the organization who have become old—not chronologically (none of us can beat that)—but in their enthusiasm, spirit, and desire to get better and improve. Not good. And let me tell you—I have seen some 20-somethings who have already made some cash, figured out how to do daily eight-and-skates, who are settling down for decades of comfort and ease, and whose attitude is antique.

I also know men and women who are several years into senior status and who are as energetic, vibrant, and motivated as my 1980 teammates. These are the players I want on my team. These are the players that win.

Members of great teams remain young in spirit and outlook.

Don't Let Your Players Get Comfortable

Coaches and managers hold a large portion of responsibility for appraising and evaluating the troops and figuring out who is getting comfortable—who is ripe to get old. If you identify a person getting old and you don't do something about it, then you are part of the problem.

That scene in *Miracle* where Herb confronted me following the shellacking we took at Madison Square Garden is based on reality. I knew and was secure that I would be the starting goalie in the Olympics. I had lost a bit of focus—I was even thinking ahead to an NHL contract and making some money. I had gotten old at 22. Herb saw this and he confronted me in the locker room following the Soviet exhibition game. He said he needed to sit me down and give Janny a look. Herb said, "No, it's my fault, Jim. I have worked you too hard. You've lost your fastball and your curveball is hanging. We are going to need something more." I went ballistic—okay semi-ballistic—telling Herb that he couldn't do that, that it wasn't right. Herb said that to keep my job I needed to get back the intensity, focus, and attitude that he knew was in me.

As a national spokesperson for W.L. Gore and its Ultimate SAAAVE public affairs campaign, it is essential for me to constantly read up on the most recent scientific and clinical developments in vascular health and endovascular repair in order for me to provide the best value to Gore. I surely don't want to get complacent and old in this project.

I'm not a scientist or doctor—but that doesn't mean I can't stay smart about what is going on in the field. Gold Medal Strategies has a research team that runs down articles and papers for me relating to the heart and arteries, as well as the newest and best ways to fix arteries and repair aneurysms. If I don't understand something then I might call a W.L. Gore field representative; or I might e-mail or call one of the surgeons with whom I work.

Some of the most gratifying work I do is on Ultimate SAAAVE. What is more rewarding than working with smart and committed people in an effort to save lives? I have had the fortune and opportunity to stand in an operating room and watch, in person, endovascular repairs and even an open-heart surgery. I sit and talk with very smart Gore personnel and medical doctors from across many different specialties. I always seek to learn more—to stay young in spirit and outlook—so that I can do a better job in educating the public.

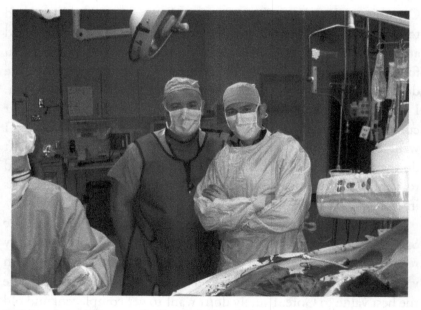

Jim, left, and vascular surgeon, Dr. Timothy Sullivan, in the operating room during an endovascular repair procedure.
Credit: Jim Craig

Staying young in spirit and outlook requires members of teams to never stop learning and to always ask questions and to be on the constant search for better ways to do things.

■ ■ ■

The Technology Challenge

One of the biggest challenges in sports, business, education, government, medicine, the military . . . you name it . . . is how to best use technology to win. It is a definite fact that if you don't stay young in spirit and outlook, then you are going to fall behind the technology curve—and that is a sure death knell to any chance you have for greatness.

My team at Gold Medal Strategies and my children, JD and Taylor, force me to stay current with technology. They coax and remind me that while I might be comfortable using an older technology, I am losing out in efficiency and productivity by not changing.

The people around me pull me out of my comfort zone.

In that I make a living speaking and writing and I am traveling frequently, it is essential that I have available and know how to use the best mobile communications technology.

I work with an advisor and techno wiz, Joe Sullivan, to make sure I am up-to-date and connected. Joe has put together and coordinated for me a system of mobile technology that connects an iPad and a Smartphone that run Microsoft Office, ACT! scheduling, and Dragon voice recognition software. Using this technology enables me to constantly learn, adapt, and make my presentations better as I travel. Joe is the husband of Lisa Sullivan, who has been my executive administrator for the past eight years, and who has been a valuable resource for me for the past 20 years.

Make the Workplace Fun—At Least Some of the Time

My mom recited to me the adage, "All work and no play makes Jack a dull boy." How true. All work and no play also wears down Jack and makes him old before his time.

I delivered a keynote address in Orlando on October 16, 2010, at the annual meeting of Physician Sales & Service (PSS), the United States' largest supplier of medical products and solutions to doctors' offices. In the audience were 700 PSS sales reps and their spouses and significant others (which brought the total attendance to about 1,200). PSS, founded in 1983, competes in a brutally competitive business which had also become an industry of immense uncertainty because of—and this is true no matter where you fall in the political spectrum—the health care bill passed in Washington, D.C. in the summer of 2010. At the time of my speech, with the midterm elections a little more than a couple weeks away, it was tough to figure out what the healthcare marketplace and industry would look like even six months down the road—never mind a year.

Yet even though the pressure was on, PSS sought, as it always did, to engender and support a corporate atmosphere in which people could enjoy themselves while competing fiercely. This is the corporate culture of PSS, and it has helped keep its workforce young, engaged, and full of energy. PSS has had almost continuous growth in the close to 30 years it has been in business—and at the same time it has held on to its top-performing reps for long periods. People like to work at PSS, and their happiness with their jobs and the workplace supports the success of the enterprise.

"We have a philosophy at PSS that we want to work hard and play hard," said Eddie Dienes, president of the PSS Physician business, and a 22-year veteran of the company. "We believe that we owe our people professional development, and the best training and education available to help themselves, and our customers. We also are committed to rewarding our people so they are motivated to perform. Our company invests in helping our employees be best-prepared to serve the needs of a rapidly-changing U.S. healthcare market. In return, our people are motivated, youthful, and the best-conditioned to achieve success for themselves, our customers and PSS."

Eddie added—"I have been with PSS since the late 1980s, and today I am more excited and enthused about the future, and as hard working as ever."

In talking and having time to meet and socialize with the PSS team in Orlando it was apparent to me that it was a team of winners with an upbeat attitude, confidence, and commitment to one another and to overall PSS success.

Caring About Your People and Your Customers Makes the Workplace Fun

Companies hire me, in part, to make the workplace fun. Hiring a keynote speaker is a big investment and I better make sure that I entertain, inspire, and, as appropriate, deliver specific and customized strategic direction. Front and center on my radar screen when preparing, on game day, and in the game itself, is to get people smiling, energized, and laughing, in order to have them leave the event with an upbeat feeling and an intent to perform better.

That is why when I practice and assemble the information I need for a speech or other presentation, I consult and communicate closely with the client. Actually, even before I get on a conference call or exchange some e-mails with the client, I like to have in hand biographical information on the people with whom I would be talking. So I see that the vice president of marketing has a bachelor's degree from Michigan—okay. On the call I might say to her—"The Wolverines did a good job against Notre Dame on Saturday. Did you watch the game?" (If Michigan didn't do so well against ND, I would make sure not to bring it up.) My staff might hand me a trade magazine bio on the president of a manufacturing firm I will be addressing—and I learn he enjoys boating. Well, I have a boat and love to get out on the ocean. Boating is something I might bring up. The executive assistant to the president used to work for John Hancock. I do a lot of work for John Hancock. "When you worked at John Hancock, did you know. . .?"

I step into my relationship with a client equipped with a lot of background information—and in my interaction with the client I continue to gather information. I also make sure to try to learn about the people and the personalities of the groups that hire me. When you care about people and you invest in their success—and they invest in you—then you help make the relationship enjoyable.

In late summer of 2010, my staff and I had a conference call with management from Wells Fargo as part of the research and preparation for a speech I would deliver for the firm. As we were about to conclude the call, Rob Meyncke, regional sales manager for Wells Fargo, said, "Jim—you haven't spoken for us yet—and this already has been the most positive experience that our group at Wells Fargo has had with a speaker."

I never "mail it in." And by never mailing it in I refuse to become complacent and to get old—and I do my job by making my appearance fun for the client and, yes, for myself.

■ ■ ■

Do you care about your employees? Do you circulate among the troops? Do you take time to learn about their personal hopes and aspirations? Do you know her husband's name? His wife's name? How many kids does he have? What are their names? How old are they?

So, Bob has a 12-year-old boy named Timmy. What does Timmy like to do? He is an artist—he likes to paint. He plays baseball; he's a pitcher. Who is his favorite baseball player?

The office can become a stodgy, old, and unhappy place when it is a cold and impersonal place. Teamwork is more than working together—it is also caring and looking out for one another. It is about showing appreciation for one another. The example can be set at the top.

For sure—the dynamic with the 1980 U.S. team was a bit bizarre—unifying in dislike of our coach and in an effort to show him that he couldn't break us and that we were better than he said we were. But I think we all understood that Herb did care about us; it was just that we had big-time problems with the tough love he administered; it was too tough and harsh a medicine.

In his own way, Herb transmitted that caring and concern from the top.

The 1980 U.S. hockey team became stronger and more effective on the ice the closer we came to becoming a family. And, sure, we were a bunch of kids—but early on we were guarded and not as inclined to be exuberant and to act like the immature and impetuous young men we all were inside. When we got to know each other better and to trust one another we began to let it out, and this released a torrent of emotion, energy, and potential that we rode through two incredible and improbable weeks in Lake Placid that resulted in us standing on top of the victory platform.

If you don't take an interest in and care about your employees, then you are not supporting an environment in which they take an interest in one another. When there is no warmth or personal engagement within an organization, then you have an automated grid and a floor of cubicles in which Bob Cratchits toil away to produce numbers and reports and products—but do so with little emotion. And if you have Bob Cratchits working under you—what does that make you? You got it. Ebenezer Scrooge.

Again—and I can't emphasize this enough—at the heart and soul of the strength of our team was our youth, energy, and emotion. It was unbridled and barely controlled—yet it supported superior strategy and tactical efficiency. When you can synthesize those elements then you have something very special on your hands.

Release the hounds and have them run at full strength—yet keep them on the path that has been structured and laid out before them.

Henry David Thoreau—a guy who lived about 35 miles northwest of where I grew up—wrote, "None are so old as those who have outlived enthusiasm." Isn't that the truth? When you don't have enthusiasm then you aren't having fun and you aren't enjoying life.

Thoreau also penned these words: "The mass of men lead lives of quiet desperation."

If you can, play the video of the U.S.–Soviet game, and you will witness an event and experience in which our play was totally absent of quiet desperation—there's not an ounce you can find. Watch it intently over and over. Evaluate the enthusiasm, effort, and the intensity. Check out the laughter and smiles (yes, there was a lot of both even before time expired). Zone in on the audacity and bombast. See us embrace and share history with each other.

I can't bottle all of that for you.

But I can show it to you and recommend it.

Dare to Be Different—Push Innovation

Allow me to continue on this Concord writer track here with a quote from Ralph Waldo Emerson: "In every work of genius we recognize our own rejected thoughts: they come back to us with a certain alienated majesty."

There are few things more dispiriting than to watch potential squandered and a super idea untried. That is a downer that will purge the youth right out of you.

I need to go back to the operating environment of our team—because I think that low PDI is so critical for giving voice to historic innovation and groundbreaking achievement. For sure, Herb Brooks was the Ayatollah; he was the boss and he could direct fear through you. But he allowed us to speak up and to be heard. Our team was an environment hospitable to difference of opinion and new ways of thinking.

The method of play that combined the North American and European-Soviet forms of hockey had been talked about and discussed for several years, but no team put it into action. Herb never got old and never stopped learning—and he felt that if he had just the right group of players, he could make it happen. The 1980 U.S. hockey team finally did what many only thought about—and look at the result. It took gumption and a supporting cast willing to go along. Heck, unless the right group had been assembled—long on youth and inexperience and short on inhibition—the revolutionary form of hockey that confounded convention and the Soviets may have only been a concept and theory, never a fact and reality.

What I find interesting is that some of the most successful and moneymaking innovations in history aren't really all that complex; it's just that someone went out, took the idea, and did something about it. I mean the Foreman Grill is nothing but a waffle iron.

On the same street that I grew up in North Easton—about a half mile away—there was this big and stately Victorian home. Living there was a guy named William Amory Parker and his wife, Elise Ames Parker. I used to walk by their house to and from school. They were nice; I waved to them and they waved back. I didn't know much about them except that they were very rich. As I later found out, in the 1920s, Mr. Parker—who was an old man when I was a kid—and some of his business partners got the idea of taking a bunch of individual stocks and bundling them together and selling them as a fund—a *mutual* fund. Simple, but brilliant. The concept caught on.

Gold Medal Strategies is located in Middleboro, Massachusetts, the heart of Cranberry Country and on the cusp of Cape Cod. One of our clients is a neighbor—the cranberry cooperative giant Ocean Spray—whose worldwide headquarters straddles Middleboro and borders Lakeville. There is much to admire about Ocean Spray—among those admirable qualities are that it is a fun place to work and it encourages idea generation and innovation from across the enterprise.

In the fall of 2010, in the midst of the difficult recession, Ocean Spray finished up its most successful year to date with $2 billion in revenue. Supporting that success is—if you will pardon the expression—a thirst for innovation and fresh ideas.

What company created the juice box? Ocean Spray. What company introduced fruit juice blends? Ocean Spray. Packaging and innovation are big moneymakers for Ocean Spray. But one of my favorite Ocean Spray innovations is a snack that I enjoy gobbling—the craisin. I like telling the story about the history of the craisin; it shares with Mr. Parker's mutual fund the identity of a simple and ingenious concept. Until the mid-1990s, Ocean Spray would pull the juice from the cranberry, leaving behind the hull of the berry, which was considered trash. Ocean Spray hired companies to haul the hulls away. Then Ocean Spray said, "Wait, let's see if we can do something with these hulls." So it did. It took the shriveled hulls, previously thought to be useless, pumped some juice into them, and—voila—the craisin.

Originally Ocean Spray marketed the craisin as a baking product that would sit in the grocery aisle next to chocolate chips and raisins. Now it pushes craisins as a snack food—where it is delivering serious cash for the company. Ocean Spray has a portfolio of more than 100 products—and the fastest-growing product in the portfolio is the craisin.

Take Care of Yourself—Be Good to Others

Staying young in spirit and outlook is more than attitude. You need to take care of yourself and be good to others. Advise those who work for you to do the same.

Take care of your mind and body; exercise and eat healthy.

Jim at Lake Placid on February 22, 2005, participating in the 25th anniversary celebration of the "Miracle on Ice".

Credit: AP Images

Take time for reflection and recreation. One of the most valuable lessons to be taken from training and competing at a high level in athletics is that rest is a vital component for making an athlete sharp and able to perform at his or her peak.

The rise and popularity of corporate wellness programs in America is a good thing—especially if people use their services and take heed of their counsel.

You can put into place all the best strategies and operations—but if you have employees who are overweight, who tire easily, and who aren't taking care of themselves, then you are at a competitive disadvantage. You can be the most talented manager or CEO in the world—but it isn't going to do much good if you drop dead from heart attack.

If you are living a healthy life, then keep at it. If you aren't living one, then start. Set up an appointment with your doctor and get a healthy routine in order.

I have a crazy schedule with long stretches of hopping on planes, taking cabs, and staying in hotels. But I work with my staff to plan and be smart about eating on the road and in making sure the places where I stay have workout facilities. Actually, in terms of exercise, whether at home or on the road, when I do my cardio-training sessions—which are usually 60-minute fast walks at an incline on a treadmill—I use that time to go over my speech notes and practice delivering the speech.

When you plan ahead and stay organized you are better able to stay away from junk food and to stay active.

Spend time with your family. I don't care how much money you make and how big a star you are in business—if you aren't spending time with your family then you are losing in the most important area of life.

Give. Volunteer. Get involved in the community. Join the Lions Club or the Garden Club. Coach youth sports. Support the local high school sports teams.

When you give and care for others you give and care for yourself. You improve the world.

Don't consume more happiness than you create.

When you take care of yourself and are good to others it makes it a lot easier to stay young in spirit and outlook.

Beyond the Ice—Other Mentors and Coaches

In Chapter 8, "Members of Great Teams Manage Through Ego and Conflict," I write about how our assistant coach and general manager, Craig Patrick, calmed the storms that broke out within our team.

Craig had all the experience and character and skills to perform that role. He was a standout at the University of Denver and played on teams that won back-to-back NCAA championships in 1968 and 1969. While serving in the U.S. Army he played on U.S. national teams in 1970 and 1971, and then went to the NHL where he played for eight years. Craig played for the United States in the Canada Cup in 1976, and was a player-coach in the 1979 World Championships in Moscow, a tune-up for his job on the 1980 U.S. Olympic team.

Craig was a member of the "Royal Family of Hockey." His grandfather, Lester Patrick, and Lester's brother, Frank, were standout professional players in the early 1900s, and later co-founded the Pacific Hockey Association. Lester Patrick went on to become a coach and then general manager for the New York Rangers. Craig's younger brother, Glenn, played in the NHL and World Hockey Association.

In the 1928 Stanley Cup finals, Lester Patrick showed just what can be achieved when you stay young in spirit and outlook.

The finals that year pitted the Rangers against the Montreal Maroons in a best three-out-of-five series. Montreal won the first game—and in the second game New York goaltender Lorne Chabot sustained an eye injury and couldn't continue. Teams didn't have backup goalies then, and Lester Patrick asked the Maroons if he could put in a borrowed goaltender. The Maroons refused. Lester Patrick had to decide what to do now. What the 44-year-old Patrick decided to do was to strap on the pads and defend the New York net himself. Patrick knew the team just needed to get through that game—and then it would have time to hire another goalie. Lester Patrick told his players, now his teammates, "You better check like hell—and boys, don't let the old man down."

Lester Patrick defended the net like a kid—and his player-teammates played inspired hockey. The game went into overtime. In the extra frame, the Ranger's Frank Boucher scored and the series was tied at a game each. The Rangers hired New York Americans goalie Joe Miller to finish the series. Miller won two games, including a shutout—and New York was the Stanley Cup champ.

Lester Patrick and how he rose to the occasion in game two of the 1928 Stanley Cup finals remains one of the legendary stories in NHL history.

■ ■ ■

As I write this, it seems that in the American workplace it is now more important than ever to refuse to grow old and to remain young in spirit and outlook—no matter your biological age.

It is vital to take on the attitude of a Lester Patrick and know that age is just a matter of attitude—and that the spirit and fire of youth can be summoned for greatness.

This is a scary time in America. The economy is terrible—it is even described as a mini-depression. Unemployment is close to 10 percent, and may be even higher because it is not factoring in people who have given up looking for work. Homes are being foreclosed on at a record rate. A higher percentage of people in America live in poverty than ever before.

One of the more depressing aspects of this downturn is that people as young as 50 are experiencing age discrimination in the workplace. Employers can deny it all they want, but the fact is it is there. Baby Boomers who have had great jobs and made great money in management and executive positions have been laid off and are having immense difficulty finding work that will pay even close to what they were making before. And even when they are willing—even eager—to take a lower-level job that pays significantly less than their previous job, they are considered overqualified.

Add an illness or other outside-the-workplace setback and the situation gets dire.

I don't make these comments from a perch or in any sort of patronizing way. Yes, my wife and I have worked hard and saved and been frugal—but we also have been blessed; we understand that. I was only 22 when I had the great fortune of being part of something special that opened many doors for me to this day. After hockey, I found employment doing something at which I had inherent ability, which I enjoyed, and at which I worked hard to succeed.

And being a member of a warm and vocal family of storytellers (indeed, my Irish brethren say that a writer is a failed talker), is there a better job than the one I hold now?

But I also recognize what is going on out there.

Staying young in spirit and outlook is more important today than ever before. Those looking for work who have been knocked down and submitted application and application and resume after resume without desired results need to fight creeping despair, boredom, and belief that the future can't get better.

It can get better—a lot better.

One of my best friends and one of the most valuable mentors in my life is Jon Luther, executive chairman of the board for Dunkin' Brands, and the guy who, starting from 2003, stewarded Dunkin' Donuts—the signature brand of the company—to stratospheric growth. Jon, 67, is as energetic, fit, focused, and young as ever. He will also tell you the story of how 17 years ago—when he was 50—the company he had owned and operated for 10 years, which bought and sold restaurant companies, went belly up. He was broke, had a wife, and two kids in college.

"It was a difficult period—and I was up against it," Jon told me. "My checking and savings account hovered between a zero balance and close to a zero balance. I knew, though, that I had responsibilities and talent and that I would be able to turn things around. I went right back at it."

Jon remained young in outlook and spirit.

Jon was hired by Delaware North to work in its airline concessions business. Jon moved fast and upward in the unit—and is widely credited with transforming boring and uninspiring food stops for travelers into fun, warm, and vibrant spots where people felt like spending money and staying for a while. Jon marshaled and directed an effort that turned the company's $17 million operating deficit into a $35 million profit. In 1997, a struggling Popeye's Chicken and Biscuits hired Jon as president. He continued his brilliant field leadership and over a five-year period presided over a company that continually increased its annual profits and became so strong that its parent company, AFC, went public in 1992. It's no wonder that Dunkin' Brands came calling.

You see, at 50 years old, Jon Luther was just warming up.

Employers need to take note. People are living longer. Sixty is the new 40. I might be wrong about that—perhaps 70 is the new 40. We are going to have to rethink 65 as a standard retirement age. Sixty-five and you should be in your prime.

Thomas Watson—for all intents and purposes the founder of IBM—ran the company until he was 82. Warren Buffett is still going strong at 79. Charles Dolan, founder of Cablevision, is 83 and the chairman of the board for the company.

Carl H. Lindner, who dropped out of school in the Great Depression to work in his family business, co-founded with his brother, in 1955, the company that would become American Financial Group, which he served as chairman and CEO until he was 85, when he turned over CEO duties to his two sons. Lindner held on to his chairman position, which he still holds at 89.

Great businesspeople remain young in spirit and outlook.

So, too, do members of great teams.

Great Teams Stay Young in Spirit and Outlook— Chapter Recap

- **Don't Let Your Players Get Comfortable:** When you get comfortable you lose energy—you become less vibrant. Keep players on their toes.
- **Make the Workplace Fun—At Least Some of the Time:** If you're not having fun then you are growing old.
- **Dare to Be Different—Push Innovation:** Doing things differently and innovating is the soul of staying young in spirit and outlook.
- **Take Care of Yourself—Be Good to Others:** It is easier to stay young when you are healthy in mind and body. Overall health includes giving to others.

8

Great Teams Manage Through Ego and Conflict

> *"The aim of an argument or discussion should not be victory, but progress."*
>
> —JOSEPH JOUBERT

It was February 22, 2005, a quarter of a century to the day of our victory over the Soviet Union at Lake Placid—and there had been no NHL hockey played all winter, actually longer than that. That's right. An irreconcilable dispute between NHL owners and players had resulted in an owner lockout of the players that began on September 16, 2004, and was still in effect more than five months later. Things wouldn't get resolved until the summer. No regular season. No playoffs. No Stanley Cup winner. It would be the first time in the history of professional sports in North America that an entire season was cancelled because of a labor dispute.

But on the 25th anniversary of the "Miracle on Ice," an incensed sports columnist named Gary Shelton, writing in the *St. Petersburg Times*, had hope for something of a season to be salvaged——and he invoked the better angels and example of the 1980 U.S. Olympic hockey team in his attempt to persuade NHL commissioner Gary Bettman and the NHL Players Association executive director, Bob Goodenow, to return to the negotiating table. Here is an excerpt from Shelton's column:

> Bring them into the room. Use force if necessary.
>
> Cuff them. Carry them. Drag them. Gag them. Drop them off. Prop them up.
>
> This is not a negotiation. This is an education. So put Bettman in this chair and Goodenow in that one. Dump the lackeys and the yes men on the floor. Just get them into the room and strap them where they sit.

Ready? Turn on the projector.

We're going to settle the silliness you have brought to hockey.

Do you recognize what you are seeing? You should. Those images rolling across the screen are members of the United States' 1980 Olympic hockey team. Look closely, guys. You can see sacrifice up there. You can see achievement. You can see the selflessness and teamwork, discipline and resiliency. Look, and you will see the pure love of hockey. You will see possibilities instead of proposals, performance instead of posturing. Pay attention.

Evidently, some of you have forgotten the things this team knew by heart.

I don't cite those words to criticize the players or the owners in the drama—many of whom I know well and respect. What I am pointing out is that we had the fortune of not tussling with money and being seduced by it—and we were able to come together and put aside our differences, work through the problems, and leave our egos at the door, so that we could do something great. We had the benefit of not being big names and not worrying if U.S. amateur hockey administrators were making money off of us. No contracts. No clauses. No fine print. Indeed, the only contract decisions with which we had to deal were to hold off signing a pro contract so that we could play in the Olympics. Our lives were infinitely simpler and less complicated.

We weren't big shots. We weren't stars. If we were going to do something great we needed each other and had to do it together. We couldn't afford to wallow in our differences to get laid low by towering egos.

We needed to manage through ego and conflict.

■ ■ ■

My teammate Jack O'Callahan recently sent to me this reflection on how we managed through ego and conflict:

> I think the ego issue was not a big part of our team's makeup or the makeup of the individuals. The one common denominator was that all the players respected what the others had done for their college teams, many if not all had been drafted by NHL teams, and we were all in the same place—whether we would ultimately be one of the final 20 players. I think Herb's leadership in setting very high team goals kept anyone from getting too ahead of themselves as individuals. The leadership that was focused, demanding, and held the players accountable kept the dynamic tight.

Jack—or "OC," as the team called him—has excellent insight in pointing out how shared challenges and a shared goal helped prevent and manage disrupting influences. In our final tune-up game prior to the Olympics—the one in which we got manhandled by the Soviets—Jack sustained a knee injury that would have kept a less tough competitor out of the Olympics. Herb and the staff had a tough choice to make: A final roster had to be submitted to the Olympic organizers before we arrived at Lake Placid. If Jack was kept on the team but couldn't skate in the games, then we would lose a vitally important defenseman position. But the right decision was made and Jack was kept on the squad. He missed the first two games of the Olympics (not the five games that *Miracle* dramatized) but, for the remainder of the games in the Olympics, he was ready, if not at 100 percent physically, then definitely at the full quotient of his normal and fiery spirit. Because OC was still a bit hobbled, in the games he did play at Lake Placid, he did not see the number of minutes he did in our pre-Olympic competitive preparation. How Jack handled his reduced playing time is testament to his willingness to check his ego at the door and to not pout, moan, or complain that he had been given a bad break. His attitude remained as positive and supportive as ever throughout the Olympics. And it goes without saying that when he was on the ice he gave it his all. I think it is poetic justice, in a way, that in one of the most famous photographs in sports history—the photo that Heinz Kluetmeier shot of the on-ice celebration after the Soviet game—OC is prominent, on his knees, his arms outstretched, his mouth open wide, and yelling for all the world to hear.

In the summer of 2009, U.S. Olympic hockey officials had OC speak to members of the squad that would represent the United States in men's hockey at the 2010 Vancouver games. In front of my teammate were not the college kids we were—not the unheralded nobodies we were in the summer before Lake Placid—but a group of rich NHL stars, not one of whom needed to play in the Olympics to earn their bona fides as a great hockey player.

But the NHL standouts listened and were respectful—and this all suggested that they had their egos in check—and it all bode well for Vancouver. When OC finished speaking, the NHL players gave him a standing ovation.

I talked to OC shortly after he gave that speech, and he told me the primary message he wanted to get through to the 2010 U.S. Olympic team was that a collection of great players was just that— a collection of great players; it wasn't necessarily a team. It would take a team to win Olympic gold. OC said he told them it had to be about team first.

The U.S. players got the message. They played together and as a team in winning the silver medal—losing in sudden-death overtime to the heavy pre-Olympic favorite, Canada.

OC and his talk to the 2010 U.S. men's Olympic hockey team—and the values he emphasized—are emblematic of the type of person he is. He is a winner on and off the ice. After the Olympics, OC had a successful nine-year career in the NHL, seven of which were with the Chicago Black Hawks and two with the New Jersey Devils. While still playing pro hockey, OC—who was accepted as an undergrad to Harvard University—purchased an options member-ship at the Chicago Mercantile Exchange and in the offseason studied and interned in the futures market. When OC retired from the NHL, he spent three years as a futures pit trader; he then launched, along with former Harvard star and NHL player, Jack Hughes, a company called Beanpot Financial Services which is a broker and dealer for institutional clients.

Jack is still a competitor. As he has told me many times, the trading pit is another arena of competition. And you need to prepare for it just as carefully and with as much focus as you would for a hockey game. You have to practice and be in condition—mentally and physically.

■ ■ ■

There would have been no "Miracle on Ice" had ego and conflict not been managed. We would have left Lake Placid with no medal at all.

More great efforts have been undone by ego left unchecked and conflict not resolved than can ever be imagined. This negative energy brings down sports teams, companies, political campaigns, armies, and even societies and nations.

But the thing is this—ego and conflict can be healthy if managed and controlled. When they are not controlled, they become a monster that eats your group from within.

Managed and controlled, ego and conflict are energy and a source of winning ideas and inspiration. Not managed and controlled, they cause people to fight each other, not the competition—and that is a formula for losing.

Ego and conflict, untamed, prevent the sharing of a dream—and they disrupt the shared dreams that are in place.

Throughout the journey of the 1980 U.S. Olympic hockey team, the team had a lot of ego and conflict percolating within. What changed in the journey, though, is that, early on, there were egos and conflicts that were sufficiently managed so we could be winners. Right from the get-go, the process of managing through turmoil was underway—but it was just a start; we all had a bit of a go-it-alone and Wild West mentality among ourselves. We weren't a team.

We got there of course. It was rough and there were many blow-ups and angry and hurt feelings; there were doubts and misgivings and many questions that had to be overcome. But we dealt with the hurt and licked our wounds—and we overcame doubt and found, together, the answers we needed to win.

We stood on top of the victory platform at Lake Placid—all 20 guys—because we were able to manage through ego and conflict. Great teams manage through ego and conflict.

Find a Buffer-A Go-Between

Curiously, and this is discussed in the chapter "Great Teams Have a Real or Invented Enemy," a primary way that ego and conflict were managed on our team was for the players to coalesce and get together to oppose our coach, the man we called the Ayatollah. He was our common enemy. When we were all together and complaining about Herb—and in unison working our tails off to prove his negative assessments of us wrong—then ego and conflict were managed in a way that created positive energy. This strategy was a bit unconventional; it also got the job done.

Herb was the enemy—and the liaison between the enemy and the players was Craig Patrick. Without Craig Patrick and the role he played, we would not have won gold. Herb was often harsh and straightforward and bitingly critical. He assigned Craig the job of acting more like a big brother to us and passing information both ways—from Herb to the players and from the players to Herb—that both sides wanted passed.

Craig did not betray the confidence of either side. Yet he had an ear to the ground on which Herb operated and on which we operated, and he was able to make suggestions and deliver advice to Herb and to the players that resulted in better communication and understanding across the organization.

Craig, a talented player and an astute hockey mind, was the right guy for this job. A hockey guy inside and out, he loved the game about as much as anyone could.

Again, as I mentioned in Chapter 7, it would be Craig's role as a player-coach in the 1979 World Championships in Moscow that would be his tune-up for his job on the 1980 U.S. Olympic team. Herb was looking ahead to Lake Placid—and the need for a smart hockey mind that would operate in that liaison capacity—when he selected Craig as player-coach for the 1979 tournament. Craig was nearing the end of his professional career, and since he absolutely could not leave hockey, the next step would be to the coaching and administrative ranks. Coaching and playing in Moscow were all part of the transition.

Remember, it was Craig Patrick—not Herb Brooks—who, in the tournament in Moscow, delivered to me the terrifying news that I would play in the next game against the fearsome Czechs.

In the summer of 1979, Craig had just hung up his competitive skates, but he still had so much of the player in him—physically, emotionally, and spiritually. He had just finished his pro and international career a few months previous. He would be 34 years old at Lake Placid while Herb would be 42. Craig had a lot more in common with the players—in terms of recent experience in hockey—than did Herb.

So as we prepared for the Olympics, and during the Olympics themselves, Craig Patrick was the buffer, the intermediary, the liaison, and sort of a sounding board as well, who diffused friction and calmed things down. In terms of hurt feelings and bruised egos, Herb wasn't in the business of tending to those and giving the warm fuzzies. Craig jumped in to handle that chore.

When Herb entered the locker room in the first intermission of the Sweden game at Lake Placid, and was about to jump ugly, *real* ugly, with Rob McClanahan, he caught my eye and gave me a wink—and then he caught Craig's eye and gave him a wink. What Herb was doing here was mitigating a bit the mayhem he was about to set off. When Herb was leaving the locker room—amid the ranting and hollering—he gave a wink to both Craig and I and said, "That oughta get 'em going." It sure did.

What wasn't shown in *Miracle* was what happened after Herb walked out. Craig Patrick then took over and calmed things down. He told us to forget about Herb and what he said—and that we had a commitment to one another—and that it didn't matter how furious we were at Herb, we had to go out and play.

Craig Patrick and Jim at 2010 Robertson Cup Banquet.
Credit: Jim Craig

In the locker room—as he frequently did—Craig played the good cop to Herb's bad cop.

If Craig hadn't done his job then and there, we would have lost our focus and almost certainly the game. And if we had started out the Olympics with a loss, the possibility of any miracle would have been erased almost as soon as we started. Craig was also the guy who took the team's message to Herb—and again this was dramatized in the movie—that he needed to hear out some of the guys regarding how unsettling and dispiriting it was with only a few weeks to go to the Olympics to keep on bringing in new players for a look.

Over and over, Craig Patrick kept the boat steady and the train on track. He does not get enough credit for the miracle.

No One Is Bigger Than Team

One of the greatest coaches and examples of a brilliant leader and true gentleman is UCLA basketball coach John Wooden. This book was in its early development stages when Coach Wooden died at the age of 99. Of all the accomplishments of Coach Wooden, all the games won, the national championships, the trophies, the awards, the most important and enduring testament to his contribution to society is what type of men the players he coached became—and how many of them adored and kept in frequent contact with him.

As he built and mentored the most dominant men's basketball program in history, he never sought to grab the limelight and make it about him; indeed, his calm and poised demeanor on the sideline was a hallmark of his coaching. And while among the greatest to ever step onto a basketball court played for him, he made sure that no player was above the interests of the team.

There is an oft-told story of how UCLA center Bill Walton, who had earned All-American status the previous year, showed up for the first day of practice the following season sporting a full beard. John Wooden frowned on beards; he wanted all his players to be clean shaven; it was something all the players had in common and it supported teamwork. Wooden told Walton that the beard had to go. "But it is my right to have a beard," responded Walton. Wooden replied, "Yes, that is right, Bill—that is your right. I respect people who stand up for their rights. And we are going to miss you." Walton shaved the beard that day. Following his playing days at UCLA, a week did not go by when Walton did not call Coach Wooden to talk.

Consider the Herb Brooks approach to dealing with the "beard" issue when building a team and managing ego and conflict. Herb, too, had a prohibition on beards—but he faced an issue because Ken

Morrow had been sporting a beard prior to being selected to try out for the team. So this is where Herb meshed pragmatism with rules—and he did it in coy fashion. He announced that there could be no beards on the team—but if you had a beard prior to being a member of the team, then you received a waiver; you were grandfathered in.

There was only one player the rule affected: Ken Morrow.

John Wooden and Herb Brooks knew that you sow all sorts of dissension in the ranks when you play favorites and allow certain players rights and privileges not accorded everyone on the team. Sure, you reward success—and it is important to have winners and losers (otherwise, why play?)—but the rules need to be the same for everyone—with the sly exception that Herb made for Ken Morrow.

Conflict also arises when the star receives all of the spotlight, is showered with adulation and media attention, and the supporting cast remains in the shadows. This conflict largely resides in the world of sports, but it can happen in any sector. I know the reality and the economics about how big money dictates where the cameras focus and who sits to take questions at press conferences—but that doesn't mean that those who support the superstars don't get miffed and disgruntled if they don't receive their due.

But the money isn't going away.

I said that the 1980 U.S. Olympic hockey team was not a Dream Team, but a Team of Dreamers. We arrived at the village in the Adirondacks largely unknown. There were no big names on the team. If there were any celebrities in international hockey at the time they were on the Soviet squad. Compare our situation with that of the 1992 U.S. Olympic men's basketball team—the original Dream Team—that arrived in Barcelona as rock stars. This collection of hoops superstars were mobbed and followed everywhere they went. Indeed, the coach of the team, Chuck Daly, said of the experience, "It was like Elvis and the Beatles together. Traveling with the Dream Team was like traveling with 12 rock stars. That's all I can compare it to."

We didn't have to deal with such interest. Traveling with our team—the Team of Dreamers—was like traveling with ... well ... 20 amateur hockey players from the United States. Early in the Olympics, every player on our team could walk through the center of Lake Placid and not command a single autograph request. Not a single request for a picture. This would change soon, of course, but for the moment we were anonymous.

Our coaching staff considered the anonymity a positive. Herb wanted it this way. No prima donnas and there would be no conflict. If the spotlight started to shine too hot and directly on one player, then our unity could be disrupted. It was only natural; we were kids who still had a lot of growing up to do—and impressionable young people can get jealous and miffed easily. Herb took criticism for handling all the media interviews himself and keeping us away from the microphones. It was suggested that he was hogging the media and public attention. This wasn't the case. What Herb was doing was minimizing the potential for big heads and overarching egos that could affect our play.

In that preventing big heads and outsized ego was a priority, Mike Eruzione was the right captain for the team. He provided the leadership and experience and competitive fire: he was the second oldest on the team and had played in college, semi-pros, and two World Ice Hockey Championships. Yet there were many players on the team who had garnered bigger headlines and accolades. This suited Herb Brooks fine; it all synched with his strategy for tamping down on the ego and getting through the conflict.

Mike Eruzione was a superior captain and leader; he was the right captain for the team. It is fitting and well deserved that Mike was the guy who scored the game winning goal against the Soviets. And let me tell you something about that goal—that shot. Mike jokes that a friend said to him, "If that shot were three inches to the left you'd be painting bridges now." It is modesty. Mike Eruzione could always score—and he put that puck where it was supposed to go at a time when we needed it to go there.

Everyone Has an Important Role

I've written about how everyone on a team needs to be accountable for themselves and for each other. Everyone has a role to play. Remember how Gary Smith, our trainer, used his wits in the Soviet game to hold back one of our players and prevent a too-many-men-on-the-ice penalty which would have left us short-handed against the most potent office on earth. And remember the role that our team physician Dr. Nagobads had in the Soviet game—timing our shifts, making sure no shift was longer than 40 seconds.

Great friends: Jim with Dr Nagobads.
Credit: Jim Craig

When everyone on the team has a role—when everyone is invested in the process—it helps manage ego and conflict. And when you do that you give yourself a better chance to win. Everyone has an important role. Respect that role. You earn respect in giving respect, in assigning respect. David Packard, co-founder of Hewlett-Packard, understood and practiced this concept. Consider this excerpt from his book, *The HP Way: How Bill Hewlett and I Built Our Company:*

> I recall the time, many years ago, when I was walking around a machine shop, accompanied by the shop's manager. We

stopped briefly to watch a machinist making a polished plastic mold die. He had spent a long time polishing it and was taking a final cut at it. Without thinking, I reached down and wiped it with my finger. The machinist said, "Get your finger off my die!" The manager quickly asked him, "Do you know who this is?" To which the machinist replied, "I don't care!" He was right and I told him so. He had an important job and was proud of his work.

Packard—who, by the way, was a heck of an athlete at Stanford University, lettering in football, basketball, and track and field—didn't have so big an ego that he couldn't, or wouldn't, recognize that a machinist was right in reproaching him for interfering with his work.

The HP Way was big on being inclusive and rewarding everyone across the company.

Establishing a culture of managing through ego and conflict begins at the top.

And, sometimes, even people with mountainous egos can manage and oversee an organizational culture that helps manage conflict. Consider mega-casino and hotel developer Steve Wynn, known as Mr. Las Vegas. Wynn, a billionaire, has an Everest-size ego for sure—but he also invests his employees with importance, respect, and responsibility. Just prior to opening his most opulent, newest, and biggest hotel-casino, Wynn Las Vegas, Wynn and his business partner, his wife, Elaine, assembled the employees of the facility. Steve Wynn said to them:

> On behalf of myself and Elaine I'd like to get something straight. As of this minute, you will be doing me a great favor, each of you that are in this room, if you will please now refer to me as Steve and her as Elaine, wherever you see me, wherever you are. There's enough Wynn plastered around this building (laughter) to last us the rest of our lives (laughter and applause).

And I gotta get you to take responsibility. And I gotta get you to feel ownership. So I say this to you. In the opening days of this hotel, and maybe weeks, I empower every one of you that comes in contact with a customer—if you find that the food was cold, or the room wasn't ready, or the reservation was wrong, or the customer was upset, or they think they should have won the bet—don't look over your shoulder for a boss. Give 'em back the chips, cancel the check—on your own (applause). You got my permission (applause). Customer satisfaction is now in your lap as well as mine.

I do a lot of business in Las Vegas, and I have stayed at every one of Steve Wynn's hotels: Wynn Las Vegas, Bellagio. The Mirage, Treasure Island, and Encore—and every hotel is run efficiently and delivers premium customer service. I keep going back.

Making sure that everyone has an important role in the organization facilitates and supports winning teamwork.

Agree to Disagree—Work It Out

Growing up in a big Irish Catholic family—you know, the one with eight kids and one bathroom, and not a lot of money, but enough—was a high-spirited and sometimes raucous experience. We could disagree and argue and get mad at one another—but we could never stop loving each other.

I learned early in life that you can't be enslaved to hard feelings, and that holding grudges usually saps more energy and inflicts more hurt on the holder than on the object of the grudge.

I also learned that some of the best resolutions, best results, and more enduring and valuable understandings are reached and achieved when people are willing to "get into it" and disagree and listen and fight for ideas and positions. When such emotional tumult is permitted and encouraged—and properly managed, even refereed—then you have an environment in which optimum potential can be achieved.

This is the type of environment in which no idea is a dumb idea—and one in which people understand that the best way to have good ideas is to have lots of ideas. Benjamin Disraeli said, "Never apologize for showing feeling. When you do so, you apologize for the truth."

Again, I go back to the value of low PDI. You know that members of our team could challenge authority – such Herb and Craig Patrick—then we had little reluctance in speaking up to one another. But here's the thing—we would speak and argue and get it out of our system and move on. You have to move on.

It's like the scene in the movie when OC and McClanahan begin to throw down—and Craig Patrick moves in to immediately break it up. Herb holds Craig back, saying, "No, let 'em go." Herb knew what would happen: OC and McClanahan would get their licks in and perhaps some noses and lips would be bloodied—but they would also blow off emotion and get through some conflict. Their teammates broke things up as soon as they hit the ice.

When OC and McClanahan were separated, Herb lays into everyone—he said that the brawl between the players looked like, and this is a wonderful Herbieism, "Two monkeys trying to hump a football." He tells us that we need to get over the regionalism and the pettiness and to start—*now*—becoming a hockey team.

We did become a hockey team. And there were many more disagreements. But we knew we couldn't dwell on the differences and needed to come together.

Get Outside Your Comfort Zone for the Team

Dave Christian was an outstanding center and scorer at the University of North Dakota: Over just two years and 78 games he tallied 70 points. One of the Fighting Sioux teams he played for made it to the NCAA championship game—a loss against a Herb Brooks-coached University of Minnesota squad. Herb knew all about Dave, his scoring, and the offensive threat he posed. And these were the talents that put Dave front and center on the radar screen of Herb and Craig Patrick as they fashioned together their recruiting sheets for our team.

Following the 1980 Olympics, Dave went on to play 18 seasons in the NHL, scoring 340 goals and 433 assists in 1,099 regular season NHL games. And here's a bit of trivia: Which player, from the moment he first stepped on to the ice in an NHL game, took the least amount of time to score a goal? That's right—it was Dave Christian, playing for the Winnipeg Jets, who scored his first goal only seven seconds after he stepped onto the ice to start his NHL career.

Like Craig Patrick, Dave Christian descended from hockey royalty. Dave's father, Bill, and uncle, Roger, played for the 1960 U.S. Olympic team that performed the first miracle on ice, winning the gold medal at the Squaw Valley games. Bill and Roger, along with Hal Bakke, founded the Christian Brothers Hockey Company, makers of the famed hockey sticks.

As a member of the 1980 U.S. team, in the run up to Lake Placid—just as he did in college—Dave played as a center. This is the position he knew and that he enjoyed—and in which he gave us high-level value. A scoring center in hockey is something like a gun-slinging passing quarterback in football: it is a position that is a lot of fun to play—especially when you are putting up points. It is not like you are mucking around and knocking heads in the interior line in football and creating opportunities without receiving much credit—or like being a checking defenseman in hockey who is not given much of a green light to rush the net. Scorers and the offense—in all sports—grab most of the glory.

As I frequently say of playing goalie, and this applies to many positions of defense in athletics, we are there to prevent scores—and oftentimes, if we are effective or perform brilliantly in shutting down our opponent, it does not generate the enthusiasm or crowd response as when the offense beats you.

In December, one of our defenseman, Bobby Suter, broke his ankle. It looked like he would still be a go for the Olympics, but it wasn't certain. Herb needed to bolster and shore up our defense—and he got the idea to not bring in another defenseman, but to keep Bobby on and to move Dave Christian to defense. This could have been a problem if less of a team player had been asked to make the switch—but Dave was a team player through and through. When Herb told Dave that he needed him to give up his glamour spot, the one that he had played with great effectiveness his entire career, and to move back to scraping up and defending along the blue line, Dave took on the job with full body and soul.

"It wasn't a big deal; it needed to be done to make us as competitive as possible," said Dave. "Plus, I had played some defense in high school; I knew what I was doing. It was all about team—nothing else."

When Jack O'Callahan got hurt only a few days before our first Olympic game against Sweden, our blue line strength was further depleted—and the earlier decision to move Dave Christian became even more vitally important.

We would not have won at Lake Placid without Dave Christian playing defense. Bobby Suter was back but the ankle was not totally healed. Against the Czechs he hurt it again and, although Bobby is as tough and hard-nosed as they come, he was further hampered and not what he was. And, of course, there was OC who was not 100 percent either.

Dave Christian did not score any goals at Lake Placid, but he had eight assists, the most on the team during the tournament, and his skating speed and ability to thwart and throw off opposing scorers was vital to our success.

■ ■ ■

It seems that the qualities and values you learn early in life that are imbued in you as a youngster—when properly nurtured—direct you to help out and think of others and act selflessly.

As I have said, none of the players on the team were poor growing up—but none of the players came from affluence either. Almost to a man, every player came from a background in which they had enough, but not much more. Self-reliance was embedded in the code of the households of all 20 players. And in many ways, those guys from the Iron Range of Minnesota almost could not help but think of team first because in the Iron Range, if people didn't think of one another, people would not survive. I mean, when the iron mining was good then people had jobs but they didn't make much money. When the iron ore got depleted, then unemployment in some areas could be like 80 percent. During the winter temperatures sometimes hit 40 or 50 below zero. That is some hard living.

I think about an Iron Range kid like Buzz Schneider, one of the nicest people you could ever meet. A solid leader, Buzz was the oldest member of the team—an elderly 25—and the only guy on the team who had played on the 1976 U.S. Olympic squad. Buzz—a member of the famed Conehead line—was from the Iron Range town of Babbitt.

Buzz was fast and a menace for defensemen and goaltenders. He scored a hat trick on Vladislav Tretiak in the 1975 World Championships. He played full out from start to finish. He gave nothing less than 100 percent 100 percent of the time.

Now I have just told you about Dave Christian, a Minnesota kid, thinking first of team and not of himself when he made the switch to defense. And then I remember reading the *Boys of Winter* and finding out something I didn't know, but which, of course, didn't surprise me. When Buzz Schneider was entering his senior year in high school hockey, and was one of the top-scoring forwards in Minnesota prep hockey, his coach told him he wanted to move him to defense. Buzz said fine, whatever the coach wanted.

Compare the self-entitled and me-first attitudes of many of today's athletes—from youth leagues up to the pros—with those of young men like Dave Christian and Buzz Schneider. Really.

As for Buzz Schneider, it seems that being able to check ego runs in the family. Buzz's son, Billy, was a multisport standout athlete and found himself as part of a casting call audition for a role as one of the players in the Disney movie *Miracle*. You'd think that Billy might have mentioned to director Gavin O'Connor who he was—or Buzz may have let O'Connor know that that kid was his son. Nope. For sure, networking was done to get Billy into the auditions—but once there he had to deliver on his own. And he did. O'Connor, who maintains he did not know whose son Billy Schneider was, selected Billy to play, well, yes, of course, Buzz Schneider.

Beyond the Ice—Other Mentors and Coaches

Back in the mid part of the twentieth century, the U.S. Military Academy at West Point (Army) had a juggernaut of a football program under coach Earl "Red" Blaik, himself a graduate of West Point, where he played football. Blaik coached the program from 1944 through 1958, compiling a record of 168-14-14, including two national championships and five undefeated seasons, with the Black Knights finishing three of those seasons with no ties.

Red Blaik—nicknamed "Colonel" by his players—was a great coach for many reasons. One reason he was such a great coach is that he studied the game exhaustively (he was one of the first to break down game films play by play) and that he cared so much about the qualities of character when selecting his teams and his coaches.

Don Holleder had the character that Red Blaik was looking for.

In 1954, Army finished 7-2 and ranked seventh in the country. The Black Knights led the nation in total offense. They had four strong running backs, a top-notch senior quarterback, Pete Vann, and Don Holleder, a junior All-America end (in the era of "two-way" players, Holleder also started at defensive end).

Planning for the following season, Blaik was up against it in terms of whom to play at quarterback. He didn't have on obvious heir to Vann. He thought it over, and arrived at a number one candidate—one who hadn't played a down in the backfield, never mind at quarterback. That candidate was Don Holleder.

It was not orthodox football thinking. Blaik knew that Holleder didn't have enough time to learn and practice to be a standout passer, but he also knew that he was a heck of an athlete and a competitor; he could bring a lot to Army's run-intensive T formation attack. Blaik knew other things about Holleder. In his autobiography, Blaik wrote that he knew Holleder "could learn to handle the ball well and to call the plays properly. Most important, I knew he would provide bright, aggressive, and inspirational leadership."

Blaik approached Holleder with his idea. He asked Holleder not to play the position at which he was an All American. He asked Holleder if we would be the team's quarterback. Blaik was right about Holleder's leadership qualities. Holleder said that for the good of the team he would do it. He would continue to play at defensive end as well. Imagine today a quarterback in NCAA Division I football playing every down from scrimmage, and mixing those downs up between QB and defensive end.

In moving Holleder from end to QB, Blaik recognized that the Army coaching staff would have to work particularly hard with, and give particularly focused attention to, Holleder so that he could run the T formation competently.

Moving Holleder from end to QB was a solution to a problem, yet it also resulted in many adjustments—for coaches and for players. In addition, the 1955 team had been depleted significantly by graduation, injury, and a player being ruled ineligible because of a disciplinary infraction.

Adding to the challenge Army faced was all the second-guessing and criticism in the press and in other sectors about Red Blaik's quarterback decision.

It was an up-and-down season for Army.

The Black Knights won their first two games, but then failed to score an offensive point in losing the next two, to Michigan and then Syracuse. Holleder took much of the blame for the losses.

The media and fans and cadets on campus were saying that Coach Blaik had made a bad personnel decision. Don Holleder went in to see Coach Blaik; he told his coach that he was aware of the widespread unhappiness with his play at quarterback. Holleder was obviously deeply bothered. Blaik put his arm around Holleder's shoulder and said to him, "It doesn't matter what anybody else thinks or says around this place. I am coaching this Army team. And you are my quarterback!"

Things got a better; the game after Syracuse was an Army win over Columbia. Up next was a solid Colgate team, which resulted in another Army win, with Holleder throwing for three scores and running for another. Then came a loss to Yale before a packed house at the Yale Bowl. A lopsided victory over a weak University of Pennsylvania squad did little to quell the boo birds.

Army (5-3) prepared for its final contest, its annual showdown with Navy in Philadelphia. Navy (6-1-1), featuring the nation's top passer in George Welsh, was a big favorite.

The night before the game, in a team meeting, Red Blaik told the team how tough it had been that season, having had to over and over walk across the field to shake the hand of the coach of the team that had just beaten Army.

Red Blaik, the "Colonel" emphasized how difficult one more of those walks would be.

"That walk tomorrow before 100,000 to congratulate (Navy coach] Eddie Erdelatz would be the longest walk I've ever taken in my coaching life," he said.

No one spoke for a few moments. Silence. Then a voice. It was the voice of Don Holleder.

"Colonel, you are not going to take that walk tomorrow."

What happened the next day at Municipal Stadium in Philadelphia?

Navy scored a touchdown its first possession but did not convert on the extra point. The Midshipmen controlled the ball most of the first half, and two more times made it the Army 20. But both times, Holleder, the defensive end, came up big, once batting away a fourth-down pass, and on the other series recovering a Navy fumble at the 13-yard line.

Army stayed on the ground and made it to the Navy one-yard line when time expired in the first half.

In the second half, Navy had the ball on the Army 20, but again lost possession on a fumble. Army responded, marching (I know, I know; an old metaphor, but with this team it fits just right) 80 yards for the TD. The Cadets converted on the PAT. It was Army 14, Navy 6.

That finished the scoring for the afternoon.

Holleder did not complete a pass in the game—although he did throw an interception.

But the scoreboard told what was important.

In the long history of Army football and the Army—Navy football rivalry, the Army victory over Navy in 1955 remains one of the program's highlights.

Don Holleder was on the cover of the following week's *Sports Illustrated*.

Some may have called "heroic" what Don Holleder did in sticking it out and succeeding at quarterback. Some may have called "heroics" what he did on the football field. Maybe, some felt, he was the "hero" of the Army—Navy game of 1955.

Don Holleder would have told you that nothing he did on the football field was heroic. Nothing he did on a football field in Philadelphia made him a hero. What Don Holleder did on a battlefield in Vietnam made him a hero.

On October 17, 1967, Major Don Holleder, who had requested to be sent to Vietnam, was killed while attempting to rescue fellow Black Lions of the Army's Second Battalion who had been ambushed in the jungle of Ong Thanh, approximately 50 miles north of Saigon. He was one of 58 Black Lions who died in the attack.

Don Holleder left a wife and two small daughters. You can find his name on Panel 28, Row 25, of the Vietnam Veterans Memorial in Washington, D.C.

Great Teams Manage Through Ego and Conflict—Chapter Recap

- **Find a Buffer—A Go-Between:** Find your Craig Patrick.
- **No One Is Bigger Than Team:** The rules are the same for everyone—and everyone must abide by them.
- **Everyone Has an Important Role:** Not every role is of the same level of importance—but every role is important on some level.
- **Agree to Disagree—Work It Out:** Through debate, conflict, and working things through you arrive at the best ideas. Enter into each conflict with the understanding of, and commitment to, respect for one another. Don't get personal.
- **Get Outside Your Comfort Zone for the Team:** Members of great teams are prepared to sacrifice personal glory and recognition for the greater good.

9

Victory—The One and Only End Game

If you lose this game, you will take it to your (expletive) grave.

—HERB BROOKS

Some may think it a bit ironic or curious after having come this far in the book that there would be a strategy titled "Victory—The One and Only End Game." I guess people might consider it a given—right? You put in a lot of hard and smart work and you follow the game plan and then you are done. You're already a winner.

Not quite. Actually, not even close.

There is one thing that athletics teaches you: that life isn't fair—there are winners and losers, champions and runner-ups, those who snatch victory from defeat and those who crumble and choke and give up big leads in the third period.

I can go on and on how grown-ups are creating a defeatist culture in which no one wins and no one loses. The truth of the matter is, in that culture, everyone loses. If America stops keeping score and going head-to-head then we might as well resign now to second-tier status on the world stage.

We came to Lake Placid in optimum physical and mental condition. We had done everything that we needed to in practice and training. All those strategies that you read about and which were described earlier in the book, we had hewed to and followed them tightly. But here's the thing—they don't award gold medals for what you do in practice.

Gold medals are won in the arena—on game day.

Jim receives his gold medal from International Olympic Committee President Lord Killanin.
Credit: AP Images

Great teams don't merely practice and train like champions—they also compete like champions.

I can't tell you how many exceptional and spirited practice players I have seen who can't produce when—for real—the puck is dropped, the ball is kicked off, or the starter's gun sounds. As well, there are some athletes who are good but not exceptional talents, but who are such intense competitors that you want them on the ice or court or field when it is crunch time.

Something parallel happens with teams. Some teams with the most talent simply don't play like champions. Or they have a wonderful run in the regular season and then can't get it together come tournament time.

While our epic upset victory over the Soviet Union justifiably receives the lion's share of interest and delivers the most goose bumps, we didn't win the gold medal by just beating the Soviet Union. We didn't win the gold medal for beating Finland. We won the gold medal for tying Sweden, and then beating Czechoslovakia, Norway, West Germany, Romania, the Soviet Union, and then Finland. A loss to any of these teams would have taken us out of the hunt for gold.

I go back to this over and over: Can you imagine if we had lost to Finland on Sunday after pulling off, arguably, the biggest upset win in sports history on Friday night? That loss to the Finns would be an eternal fount of head-shaking, soul-searching, and teeth-grinding for the team—and the American public would have had every right to feel let down.

Many don't know or don't remember that when we left the ice after the second period of the Finn game, and we were losing 2-1, there was booing coming from the crowd—and it wasn't directed at our opponents. If you didn't know this, you might be shocked. Perhaps you are even upset that Americans could boo us after what we had done in the tournament. I don't have a problem at all with the discontent of the fans. General George S. Patton had it right: "America loves a winner"—and as Herb told us after beating the Soviets—"You haven't won anything yet." We weren't winners—yet.

The United States had been taking it on the chin for a decade; it was tired and dragging. When we knocked off the Soviet hockey team—exemplars of the mortal enemy of Uncle Sam—we plunged a syringe full of adrenaline and happy into the arm of a nation. To have brought America to such heights and not close the deal would have cheated a couple hundred million people.

We needed to beat Finland and close the deal.

■ ■ ■

Is the U.S. men's hockey team's victory over the Soviet Union at Lake Placid the biggest upset in sports history? I'm not sure. Have you ever heard of the "Miracle in the Grass"? That was the name of the crazy 1-0 upset authored by the U.S. men's soccer team over England in the first round of the 1950 World Cup played in Brazil. At the time, U.S. soccer was just in its infancy, and those early days were mostly a record of losing heavy; in its previous seven international matches prior to its World Cup meeting with the Brits, the U.S. national team had lost all its games by a combined score of 45-2. Britain was a world power and a 3-1 favorite to win the World Cup. The odds for the Americans to win were 500-1. Like the Soviet Union hockey squad we faced, the English team was for all intents and purposes a professional team. The U.S. team competing in Brazil was made up of guys who played soccer part-time and held day jobs, which included a high school teacher, a hearse driver, a dishwasher, and a mail carrier.

You think we faced long odds. That U.S. soccer team was a 100-1 underdog to England. But somehow . . . some way . . . the Americans won. Truly mind-boggling. So why is the "Miracle in the Grass" not that well known? One of the reasons, of course, is that it happened 30 years before the "Miracle on Ice." As well, there was not the political and current events drama surrounding the soccer game that circulated around our game. Another big reason, though, is that the United States lost its next match, 5-2, to Chile and it did not make it out of the first round. No American men's team would qualify for the World Cup for another 40 years.

The U.S. soccer victory over England in 1950 was big. But the team did not go far in the tournament. Herb Brooks might have said—and I know this seems harsh—that that team really didn't win anything.

Winning is everything, even if you do so by only three-hundredths of a second. Three-hundredths of a second was the margin of victory for American swimmer Michael Phelps in the 100-meter butterfly final at the 2008 Beijing Summer Olympic Games. In winning the event, Phelps tied Mark Spitz's record of seven gold medals in a single Olympics and kept alive Phelps's quest—ultimately a successful quest—to break the record in winning eight gold medals.

Who finished second in the 100-meter butterfly at the Beijing games? My point exactly.

■ ■ ■

What good is it when you build a sales force if you hire the smartest people, provide them with the best training, pump up their confidence, pay them handsomely, and treat them to pizza on Friday, if in a year's time neither profits or sales are up? Is it enough that you are running a nicely functioning ship?

There has to be a goal in front of you—an Everest-like summit that you need to reach. Dragons you need to slay. Enemies you have to thump. Critics you need to silence.

Then you need to actually reach and slay and thump and silence.

This book didn't discuss and teach the components and qualities of just being competitive, or being good, or very good—but about being great. In teaching and coaching greatness, I used an overachieving hockey team as the foundation curriculum and syllabus. And I paired those lessons and examples with achievement inside and outside of athletics.

I do believe, though, that among the most sublime and inspirational—and instructive—examples of team greatness is the one on which I played. None of us were great unto ourselves. As I have said and written, Lake Placid and 1980 were not wanting for individual greatness; there was a guy named Eric Heiden who made sure of that. We needed each other for greatness. We reached greatness as a team. Self-evident you say? I don't think so. To those who have their values and priorities in order, yes. But far too many coaches and athletes don't appreciate the essence of teamwork—relying on and being there for one another.

Really.

After the Miami Heat succeeded in bringing LeBron James and Chris Bosh on board to join Dwayne Wade—this following the nauseating and protracted media spectacle of Lebron and "The

Decision"—sports fans were treated to that "Welcome Party" circus of James, Bosh, and Wade dancing and prancing amid pulsating lights, smoke, and noise. I had questions when watching this impressive, if off-putting, show: Where was the rest of the team? Is the Miami Heat going to put just three players on the court?

I know … I know … money and media dictate everything. Yet even if the Miami Heat manages to win it all in 2011, I am not sure it will learn much about optimum teamwork.

Compare the party in Miami to what I make sure everyone knows was my favorite memory of the 1980 Winter Olympics—the podium, the awards ceremony. After the Star Spangled Banner was finished playing, we—all 20 of us—watched Old Glory get raised a little bit higher than the flag of the Soviet Union.

Each step of the podium is designed to accommodate one person—either the individual who won, or in the case of team, the one person representing the team. Our one person was our captain, Mike Eruzione. As the national anthem played, Mike stood at rapt and respectful attention with his hand over his heart. We did the same standing shoulder to shoulder and behind him. When our national anthem concluded, Mike did a double fist clench and arm-raise in jubilation, and then he turned to us. He looked at us—and we looked at him. And it was something cosmic, psychic, and emotional all at once. He then did something that isn't done in team awards ceremonies in the Olympics: He waved us all toward him, and pointed to the small area around him. We kind of started walking toward the podium—and then we started running. We were going to get on that top step—all of us—at once. We'd come that far together and we needed to be on that podium together.

I know that other winning teams don't do this in the Olympic medal ceremony—but we weren't just any team.

ABC TV sportscaster Al Michaels said that in looking at us, he wondered how we all got on to that little platform. "Maybe that was a miracle too," said Michaels. "They had become so close, and bonded so tightly."

Herb Brooks said of the scene—"That was the final verse, chapter—end of the story right there. It was a love affair."

It sure was.

February 22, 1980. Lake Placid, N.Y. The clock strikes 00:00. We beat the Soviets.

Credit: Photographer: Focus on Sport/Getty Images

I think this is why our version of "Victory—the One and Only End Game," continues to inspire so many people and so many teams. Our team truly exemplified what it meant to rely on and need every single player—and to have every single player doing his job expertly with optimum passion—and then to commit that expertise and passion to a seamless and coordinated delivery.

Of course, our team was fortunate that many exceptional and gifted storytellers took our team as their subject.

The 2004 Boston Red Sox watched *Miracle* in the clubhouse prior to their historic seventh game of the American League Championship Series against the New York Yankees. University of Alabama football coach Nick Saban had his Crimson Tide watch *Miracle* the night before its national 2010 BCS National Championship game against Texas.

Brandi Chastain said it was when watching our Olympic victory as a young girl that she became inspired to chase greatness in soccer.

It isn't just internationally-known sports teams and individual superstars who receive inspiration and motivation from our team.

A few years ago, the boys' basketball team for the high school I attended, Oliver Ames High School, entered the season without high hopes. The Oliver Ames Tigers squad, which was coached by my childhood friend, did not have the talent of many of the teams in its own league. But the team had something going for it in the way of chemistry, commitment, and passion. It won games over teams with more talent. It won the league crown that season. In the locker room prior to the game in which it would clinch the league title, a fan who had graduated from our school 15 years earlier spoke to the team in the locker room, and he told the Tigers that it was like the 1980 U.S. Olympic hockey team—and that maybe it didn't "have the best players, but it had the right ones."

It is not just in sports that our victory offers a helping hand.

I received an e-mail from a successful businessman in the San Francisco area who told me that, as a young man, he had been down on his luck with a wife and two kids and he was barely making enough to support his family. He was hurting. He told me how he followed our team and with each victory he secured new hope—and that the victories over the Soviet Union and Finland invested in him all sorts of hope and belief in new possibilities. Soon after the Olympics, he was hired as an entry-level employee at a telecommunications firm. It would be the start of a highly successful career in the industry for this gentleman—and today he is a senior executive, still in telecom.

It was May 2008 and I was up in Syracuse, New York, to deliver a speech to Aspen Dental, a large multistate network of dental offices and dental services. After the speech, a dentist introduced himself. He was born and lived in Lebanon until his family moved to the United States, the Houston area, in the summer of 1979 when he was about to begin seventh grade. Within a few months, U.S. citizens were taken hostage in Iran. He told me that, while there was nothing particularly hostile from his classmates—after the hostage-taking he was asked if he was an Iranian—he dealt with a little coldness from the other kids. He felt somewhat isolated.

Then came the 1980 Olympics—as he recalled and talked about this with me, tears came to his eyes—and he and his classmates, together, watched and followed our team and its victories and our winning of the gold.

"It was during the 1980 Olympics and what you guys did that I became an American," he said.

Victory is not everything. But it is essential to greatness.

I think when victory is achieved—when it is attained honorably and fairly—it is one of the most noble and enriching and important experiences.

I would like to leave you with some final thoughts on victory—the one and only end game.

Define Victory

In the early part of this chapter I may have seemed a bit harsh and unsympathetic, and not open to other forms of victory than that recorded by who wins on the scoreboard or who is the fastest and strongest. I know, of course, that victory can be defined and measured in many different ways. But it is also true that in the case of the 1980 U.S. Olympic hockey team, the only acceptable victory was a gold medal.

Someone who suffers a terrible injury and is told she will never walk again—and manages to put aside the crutches and step out of a wheelchair—is as great and accomplished a champion as any Olympic gold medalist. Someone who had battled the bottle and is successful staying sober is a champion. Every mother and father who works hard and brings up a family and imparts to his or her children sound morals and values is a victor.

I remember how scary it was when I first tried to earn money as a public speaker. I was terrified. But I got in front of a crowd. Just making it to that podium was a victory for me.

Everyone who faces their fears and stands them down is a winner—and achieves victory.

Everyone who fights valiantly to overcome physical and mental suffering achieves victory.

In this book I tried to teach and prescribe lessons and strategies for team greatness. I believe you need to set the bar very high and to work smart and hard in order to achieve greatness.

There are many forms of victories. The thing, though, is to get your team together and to establish a lofty goal and to deal honestly with one another in striving for that goal. You need to get a buy-in from everyone. What good is going for victory if victory means something different to different people?

I love that saying—"If you don't know where you are going, any path will get you there."

You need to set a timeline and yard marks to achieve on your quest. You can celebrate making it to the yard marks—but the ultimate goal always needs to be in mind. What represents the end zone? You can't rest until you reach it; you can't resign yourself to good enough.

About three years ago, a gentleman interviewed me for a book he was writing on successful people, about what they considered were the building blocks and important elements to success. He was a driven person, an achiever: he was a CPA who then tackled law school in his early 40s and earned his law degree. He was energetic too—traveling around the country to interview people.

While he was interviewing me he told me that he had a goal to lose weight.

"How much weight?" I asked him.

He really wasn't sure.

"When will you lose this weight by?" I asked.

Not sure about that either.

What I'm saying here is if someone as accomplished and hard-working as this gentleman doesn't establish concrete goals and measures for something as important as weight loss and his health—then how easy is it for anyone to get off track in pursuing victory?

I was in the airport in San Diego and I saw a young man, a U.S. Marine, the best and bravest of this nation. He looked a bit in distress. He was juggling his ticket and some other papers. I walked over to him and I asked if I could help. Here was a young man to whom I would cling to save me in a life or death situation, and he was out of his element and having problems. He thought he was going to miss his flight and he wasn't sure about his gate and all that. I calmed him down and I helped him get things in order. He thanked my profusely. He made that flight—and he got in touch with me via e-mail a few days later to thank me again. We have stayed in touch.

You take care of things one step at a time. Get things in order. Plan your next step. Then follow the plan.

These elements are essential to victories—great and small.

It's just the magnitude and dimensions that are different.

What Will You Do with Your Victory?

I had a speech for John Hancock back in 2007. After the speech, as is my custom, I took questions from the audience. Someone asked what Ralph Cox, the final person cut from the team, did after hockey. I was happy to tell the questioner that Ralph has done incredibly well in business—indeed his net worth might he higher than anyone else on the team. I also said that everyone on the team has gone on to be successful outside of hockey. I added with a smile, "No one is resting on his laurels on what he did 30 years ago. Only Mike Eruzione and I do that."

In truth—in one way or another—the victory of the 1980 U.S. Olympic team has had an impact and benefitted every player in many different ways. It is encouraging that all the players recognize they are custodians of a wonderful legacy and they enjoy sharing that legacy with others. Yes, I make a very good living speaking—with a considerable amount of the material I deliver being "Miracle on Ice"-focused—but I also make sure to donate and volunteer to causes in which the miracle and the telling of the miracle can enhance lives.

What I have done with my role in our victory is make a living and support my family by helping people and organizations reach their potential. I am beyond blessed and fortunate.

What will you do with your victory? If you achieve greatness—what then?

Share your success with others. Teach others the key to victory and to securing greatness. I believe one of the most telling barometers of how exceptional an athletic coach is, is how many of his or her players go on to teach and coach. Their mentor has inspired them to pay it forward.

Did you know that when Bill Belichick gets done with the Patriots and pro football he might go and take over a small college football program? Bill is a man driven to win and achieve greatness. He also is someone who will not leave this earth—and I think his father will continue to inspire him in this quest—without establishing himself as a master teacher for all time.

Bill Gates founded and oversaw the greatest software company on earth. Still only in his 50s, he and his wife are using the money and influence that greatness produced to donate billions to improving the lives of the less fortunate.

My good friend Jon Luther led and coached great teams at Popeye's Chicken & Biscuits and then Dunkin' Brands. Jon always made sure that his winning teams were more than just delivering value to customers and making money for the corporation. Jon always wanted his winning and great teams to give back and do well.

You can do well by doing good.

Doing good works completes your life.

I experienced first-hand the strength and fulfillment one receives from giving and helping when I participated in a fundraiser for my nephew, Craig Charron, who was 42 when he was diagnosed with stomach cancer in January 2010. He was living in Rochester, NY, with his wife and four children, including a newborn.

Craig was a fixture in the Rochester area, active and involved in several civic causes. Craig had been a standout scorer in the American hockey league, playing for the Rochester Americans, commonly called the Amerks. When he was just a kid, he became like a son to me when his mother, my older sister, died from cancer when she was only 40.

When word got out that Craig was sick, the Amerks and Rochester area rallied to support him and his family. Among the benefits the Amerks and people of the area organized and got behind was one held the summer following his diagnosis; the event included a golf outing, hockey game, and an autograph signing session. I participated in the benefit, as did Mike Eruzione and other Olympians, present and past NHL players, and business people I have met and with whom I have worked through my speaking and appearances.

The benefit was a success and provided much needed assistance to the Charrons.

Craig fought hard before succumbing to the disease on October 19, 2010, about a month prior to his 43rd birthday. He left his wife, Wendy, and four children, ages 13, 12, 9, and 11 months.

Many good and hard-working people are continuing to give tremendously of themselves to help Craig's family. I will continue to be involved in these efforts.

There are those great teams—like medical and scientific research teams—whose greatness would, unto itself, be all the good a team could hope to achieve. Yet even in these cases we see doctors and scientists who seek to share their wisdom and the lessons from their victories so that more great teams can be built. They intend to pull greatness out of others.

It all goes back to legacy.

Why does your victory matter?

When you think bigger and you live a life that has positive consequences for others, then greatness becomes more of a possibility.

The journey of the 1980 U.S. Olympic hockey team and its victory at the 1980 U.S. Winter Olympics at Lake Placid, NY is a testament, playbook, tutorial, and inspiration for all who seriously desire to win and be victorious.

I hope this book and our example will help you find and achieve greatness.

Victory—The One and Only End Game—Chapter Recap

- **Define Winning:** What does winning mean to you and your team? You have to be in agreement on the end game. What are the yard marks to be achieved on the journey?
- **What Will You Do with Your Victory?:** Victory unto itself is hollow. There is always a greater good for which the power and influence of your victory can be enlisted and directed.

INDEX